Southern Literary Studies
Louis D. Rubin, Jr., Editor

FAULKNER'S COUNTRY MATTERS

ALSO BY DANIEL HOFFMAN

An Armada of Thirty Whales
Paul Bunyan: Last of the Frontier Demigods
The Poetry of Stephen Crane
A Little Geste and Other Poems
Form and Fable in American Fiction
The City of Satisfactions
Striking the Stones
Broken Laws
Barbarous Knowledge: Myth in the Poetry of Yeats, Graves, and Muir
Poe Poe Poe Poe Poe Poe Poe
The Center of Attention
Brotherly Love
Hang-Gliding from Helicon: New and Selected Poems, 1948–1988

EDITED BY DANIEL HOFFMAN

The Red Badge of Courage and Other Stories
American Poetry and Poetics
Harvard Guide to Contemporary American Writing
Ezra Pound and William Carlos Williams

Faulkner's Country Matters

FOLKLORE AND FABLE IN YOKNAPATAWPHA

Daniel Hoffman

Louisiana State University Press
Baton Rouge and London

Copyright © 1989 by Daniel Hoffman
All rights reserved
Manufactured in the United States of America
First printing
98 97 96 95 94 93 92 91 90 89   5 4 3 2 1

Designer: Rebecca Lloyd Lemna
Typeface: Trump Mediaeval
Typesetter: G & S Typesetters, Inc.
Printer and Binder: Thomson-Shore, Inc.

Library of Congress Cataloging-in-Publication Data

Hoffman, Daniel, 1923–
    Faulkner's country matters : folklore and fable in Yoknapatawpha /
Daniel Hoffman.
        p. cm. — (Southern literary studies)
    Includes index.
    ISBN 0-8071-1562-2 (alk. paper)
        1. Faulkner, William 1897–1962—Knowledge—Folklore, mythology.
    2. Fables, American—Southern States—History and criticism.
    3. Literature and folklore—Southern States.   4. Yoknapatawpha
County (Imaginary place).   5. Southern States in literature.   6. Oral
tradition in literature.   7. Country life in literature.
    8. Folklore in literature.   I. Title.   II. Series.
    PS3511.A86Z789   1989
    813'.52—dc20   89-32484
                                                                  CIP

CONTENTS

PREFACE

A friend, on a recent trip, found herself seated beside a Korean professor eager to try out his English. "After a time," she writes, "he asked what I did for a living. I have difficulties explaining even to Americans just what a folklorist does, so, enunciating carefully, I told him I studied old customs, traditions, and music of different groups; that it has to do with searching for the character of a people or a region, and that this field of study is called 'folklore.' 'Ah, yessss!' he exclaimed, 'Very popular in Korea. Know well this writer William Folklore.'"

That is a confusion not likely to be made in this country. True, it has long been acknowledged that Faulkner owes much, or at least something, to oral folktales and folk speech; there are a number of excellent articles on this theme, going as far back as those by John Arthos, "Ritual and Humor in the Writings of William Faulkner" (*Accent*, 1948), and T. Y. Greet, "Theme and Structure in Faulkner's *The Hamlet*" (*PMLA*, 1957); several more-recent studies are cited in my text. But for all of them the exact relationship between Faulkner and his presumed sources in folklore proves inexact, generalized; and most concern his debt not to oral tradition but to the writings of antebellum humorists. Everyone agrees that Faulkner was exposed to a lively oral tradition, although none who heard him listen to or tell such tales as that tradition conserves ever took note of the fact.

There are several reasons why this connection has been inadequately explored. First is the need to know what one is looking for: most literary scholars are not folklorists and have only a general notion of the cultural riches and burdens of folk tradition, its stylistic characteristics, its formal attributes that a writer might appropriate for his own purposes. Further, one must know where to look, since the written records of folklore are notoriously sporadic, and many records that purport to be genuine are in fact not so. Folklorists, for their part, are likely to concentrate upon the conventional classifications of their materials, so their contribution to Faulkner studies is largely taxonomic, the collection and identification of motifs, phrases, and the like.

Perhaps the most significant difficulty is the ways that Faulkner both revealed and obscured his debts to folktale, as to most of the other sources from which he borrowed or stole elements for his fiction. At times he uses folk motifs, such as trickery or comic exaggeration, in the traditional ways; but in his work folktale plots are also stood on their heads or turned inside out, while folk-based characters may act in ways opposed to their traditional roles. It is not that Faulkner is covering his tracks; rather, his imaginative mastery of the life of his invented county demands sardonic and ironical reversals of convention, for convention, in Faulkner's view, is often a false guide to understanding.

Investigating what I call fable in Faulkner's novels requires consideration of the ways his stories are told through folktale paradigms, rituals, and myths. Folktale models can be used either to provide comic depth to the depiction of fictive reality or, contrarily, to merge with ritual and myth in the presentation of universal, timeless cultural patterns. Similarly, rituals can be either social conventions depicted realistically, such as the intricate codes of gambling, duelling, and horse trading in *The Unvanquished* and *The Hamlet,* where they function as rites of intensification, or the codified actions by which established social values can provide the entry into sacred mysteries, rites of passage through which a candidate for the knowledge of visionary truths is initiated into his destiny.

The forms of Faulkner's fictions are always problematical, for he never repeats the structure of one novel in another, and all are expedient, pragmatic, experimental efforts to hold together under great pressure themes, fables, and characters not in obvious symbiosis. Faulkner's famous complexity requires that we learn to read each of his books anew, on its own terms. I hope that by approaching the precincts of Yoknapatawpha County on the slantindicular I may be able to show evidence of the novels' structures, their internal connections and coherencies, thus far overlooked despite the many attempts before mine to survey Faulkner's work.

I have had it in mind to approach Faulkner in this manner for a long time. I hope that the approach I have worked out in three earlier books[1] will prove feasible in this one; indeed, this was originally intended to be the conclusion of *Form and Fable in American Fiction.* Two brief passages from the opening of that book will suggest its contents and the approach I plan to use in this study:

The American author who would use this lore [native folk traditions] may either deal with it for its own sake, accepting its creations and its values, or he may view the heroes of native folk experience as one end of a cultural tug-of-war in which the other end of the rope is grasped by the heroes of European tradition. The former option leads to regionalism, the latter to a much more powerful literature. For, if I may extend the image, the rope that is drawn taut between Ben Franklin, the Yankee, the Kentucky Screamer, and Johnny Appleseed on the one side and Adonis, Prometheus and Christ on the other, in its very length and tension represents the continuity of culture and the struggles of history. The ties that bind both together can be cut or burst asunder only by main force or reckless daring. Yet it is the American hero's destiny to try to break those ties. It is his fate to endure the consequences of their breaking. . . .
The strains of optimistic comedy and the mystery of the supernatural provide American literature with a cast of characters; the plots of a thousand folktales; themes of man's relation to individual man, to society, and to those forces—both the divine and the demonic—beyond man's power. . . . These folk traditions provide a rhetoric and vocabulary of comedy and, with the rudimentary structures of legend and myth fleshed and clothed in native conditions and local circumstances, they help to express man's deepest spiritual quests. Among our writers of first rank, Hawthorne, Melville, and Twain found in these traditions

1. *Paul Bunyan, Last of the Frontier Demigods* (Philadelphia, 1952; rpr. Lincoln, Nebr., 1983), *Form and Fable in American Fiction* (New York, 1961), and *Barbarous Knowledge: Myth in the Poetry of Yeats, Graves, and Muir* (New York, 1967).

valuable patterns of a 'usable past' and, in *The Blithedale Romance, Moby-Dick,* and *The Confidence-Man,* of a 'usable present' as well.[2]

A reading of Faulkner was to have provided the twentieth-century flowering of these traditions as the conclusion to *Form and Fable.* But the writing took years, and I had to decide to publish before I perished, and so postponed the Faulkner section to a later day. Other projects intervened, and it was not until a few years ago, when I took the opportunity to reread, and then teach, Faulkner's works again, that the determination arose to finish my uncompleted task. In the event, dealing with only three of his novels led to a book in itself, a sequel, which this is.

The three works I have chosen for this discussion are *The Unvanquished, The Hamlet,* and *Go Down, Moses.* True, there are folkloric elements and myths to be found in others of Faulkner's novels, but these works most attracted me because of the centrality to their structures and themes of their reliance upon prototypes and archetypes I wished to identify and the uses of which intrigued me. Further, these three works raise formal problems I hope my close readings will help lay to rest. These books have struck many readers as having been cobbled together from Faulkner's short stories. There are those who call into question their integrity as novels, noting the shifting narrative points of view, seeming diffusions of focus, and discontinuities of various sorts. Scrupulous comparisons have been made of the texts of the finished books with those of the anterior tales to determine what changes in language, characterization, incident, and emphasis resulted when Faulkner incorporated his short fictions into his larger ones.[3] The fact that his publisher entitled the last of these books *Go Down, Moses and Other Stories,* but later, at the author's insistence, deleted the final phrase, has been debated, and critics have devised new terms to explain what unity they find in this book, and what connections may be discovered between its constituent parts.

2. *Form and Fable in American Fiction,* 9, 16.
3. *Vide* James Farley, *The Making of* Go Down, Moses (Dallas, 1972); Joanne V. Creighton, *William Faulkner's Craft of Revision* (Detroit, 1977).

But such questions as these raise the further, or prior, question of why we should query the unity of three works by an author who had already composed such triumphs of complex organization and subtle interconnection of parts as *The Sound and the Fury, As I Lay Dying,* and *Absalom, Absalom!* The assumption that Faulkner didn't know how to remake his tales into novels, yoking by violence his stories from *The Saturday Evening Post, Scribner's,* and other magazines, is on its face untenable. What is lost in such discussions is a realistic sense of Faulkner's situation as a working writer. We demand of him the constant production of masterpieces, but his life required the paying of overdue bills, making a free-lance living, and so he had to devise marketable pieces of his *Comédie humaine.* Sometimes the marketable pieces—the short stories—by the vitality of the characters he had imagined and the resonance of their actions, suggested to him that they be expanded, combined, revised into larger entities, becoming, in time, for instance, *The Unvanquished.* To dismiss this work as a slick or lightweight performance because its *disjecta membra* first appeared in a mass magazine leads readers to overlook the ways these stories were rewritten and fitted together into the book itself. That Faulkner published as magazine stories early drafts of chapters from *Go Down, Moses* has nothing to do with the integral structure of the work as a novel.

Henry James called the novel "that baggy monster"; whatever it is, the novel is not a bottle of predetermined shape into which the juice of inspiration must be poured. A novel is necessarily an empirical experiment in form. The experimental form Faulkner uses in these three works, especially in *The Unvanquished* and *Go Down, Moses,* is one he first saw demonstrated by his early mentor, Sherwood Anderson. In *Winesburg, Ohio,* Anderson devised the prototype of a series of stories, seemingly independent yet interlinked, comprising a whole greater than the sum of its parts. Analysis of these Faulkner novels will show that they are cunningly made; the structure of connected stories is neither random, jerry-built, nor incomplete, but a carefully fashioned design in which characters develop and themes are ramified and presented in their full complexity. The reader is constantly challenged to interpret evidence the protagonists accept as the grounds of their lives, and the histories of the characters are subsumed in the novelistic forms that Faulkner has devised.

It may be inferred that the present study uses historical, contextual, and formal analyses, close readings of the actual texts; it does not participate in deconstruction, reader-response theory, or other current fashions of devalorizing the text by limiting interpretation to the way it may be made to support a theory— whether of linguistic self-sufficiency, economic determinism, or anything else. Neither does this examination of Faulkner proceed from a contemporary sense of grievance, perceived injustice in the treatment of race or sex, to be assuaged at the expense of the integrity of fiction. I shall address Faulkner's treatment of women and of black-white relations by trying to analyze and understand precisely what his characters in their predicaments represent, bearing in mind the cultural situation in which they were imagined and in which Faulkner lived and in which we live who receive his images.

Each of the recent aberrations of critical discourse proceeds from the critics' having lost their awareness of history: the history of our culture, the history of literature, and the history of the self. The Muses, as everyone knows, are the daughters of Zeus and Mnemosyne. All literature comes into being as the gift of the gods, fertilizing memory. It is criticism in the absence of memory that leads to the devaluation of text and the aggrandizing of commentary, to the substitution of the reader for the writer as the author of the novel. A writer such as Faulkner can be comprehended only by readers possessing a sympathetic historical imagination to complement his own.

The editor of a recent anthology of Faulkner criticism notes that "the 'truth' of Faulkner can never be known except as it is fashioned by his interpreters," and he speaks of "the transformative violence by which Faulkner has been remade in our time." Yet, having surveyed this recent criticism and made his choices, Richard J. Brodhead finds it necessary to observe "an almost total suppression of interest in where his work came from and what it effected . . . we need to know more about Faulkner's relation to the context of literature."[4] The texture of Faulkner's work makes it resistant to the simplisticism of any single theoretical approach. Writing in the wake of Conrad, Joyce, the Symbolist poets, and T. S. Eliot, as well as in emulation of Balzac and Dickens, Faulkner expresses the complexity of modernist sensibility. At the same time, as I hope to show, his work is deeply rooted in the American imagination both high and low: in his creative and original appropriations from folklore, fables, and myths, and in his development of the tradition of the great experimental romancers of our nineteenth century, Hawthorne, Melville, and Mark Twain. I hope my readings of Faulkner will add to our awareness of "where his work came from," "what it effected," and its "relation to the context of literature."

4. Richard J. Brodhead, "Introduction: Faulkner and the Logic of Remaking," in Brodhead (ed.), *Faulkner: New Perspectives* (Englewood Cliffs, N.J., 1983), 15, 16, 18.

ACKNOWLEDGMENTS

Writing this book has placed me under obligations I record with as much pleasure as gratitude. The John Simon Guggenheim Foundation granted me a fellowship, and the University of Pennsylvania a sabbatical in 1983–84 that made possible much of my research. I owe thanks for early encouragement to Joel Conarroe, then Executive Director of the Modern Language Association, and to Richard Harter Fogle, R. W. B. Lewis, and Lewis P. Simpson. On visits to Faulkner's home town and alma mater, the University of Mississippi, genial hospitality, good conversation, and research help were offered me by Evans Harrington, John Pilkington, and George Boswell. William Ferris, Director of the Center for the Study of Southern Culture, generously gave me access to his own unpublished study of horse trading, a folk tradition prominent in *The Hamlet*. Librarians, too, extended courtesies essential for my study; I am indebted to those at the Library of Congress, the Mississippi State Archives in Jackson, the University of Mississippi, the New York Public Library, the University of Pennsylvania, and Swarthmore College. I thank Liliana Underwood for research assistance and Patricia Roberts for help in preparing the book for the press. Its first readers, Louis D. Rubin, Jr., and my colleagues Romulus Linney and Robert Regan, gave my typescript the blessing of their encouragement. I am grateful for their valuable suggestions.

Several excerpts from this book have had prior publication. I thank the editors and publishers of the books and magazines listed here for their hospitality to my essays and for permission to reprint them. The first section of Chapter I, "How to Tell a Story," appeared in the *Gettysburg Review* (Spring, 1989); the second, "History as Myth, Myth as History," in J. Gerald Kennedy and Daniel Fogel (eds.), *American Letters and the Historical Consciousness* (Baton Rouge, 1987). In Chapter IV, "'Was' and

Uncle Adam's Cow" was given as a lecture at the Yoknapatawpha Conference, University of Mississippi, July, 1984, and appeared in Doreen Fowler and Ann J. Abadie (eds.), *Faulkner and Humor* (Jackson, 1986), reprinted here by courtesy of the University Press of Mississippi; "The Last of the Chickasaws" appeared in *Shenandoah* (June, 1989); and passages in "Dispossessed of Eden: 'The Bear'" are adapted from a lecture on "The Bear" given for the Voice of America and published in Hennig Cohen (ed.), *Landmarks of American Literature* (New York, 1969), reprinted by courtesy of the editor and Basic Books, Inc.

Thanks are due Random House, Inc., through whose courtesy brief passages are quoted from the Vintage editions of William Faulkner's copyrighted novels: *The Unvanquished* (1938, rpr. 1966), *The Hamlet* (1940, rpr. 1956), and *Go Down, Moses* (1942, rpr. 1973).

Faulkner's Country Matters

I

FOLKLORE, FORM, AND FABLE

HOW TO TELL A STORY

Reading through the sketches written for the New Orleans *Times-Picayune* in 1925 by the twenty-seven-year-old William Faulkner, one senses, in most of them, a talent searching for its métier. In these "Mirrors of Chartres Street," as the young author called them, are depictions of local characters in the Vieux Carré, bootleggers and their girls, racing touts—here Faulkner trying to be a local colorist, there a Southern Damon Runyon. A few pieces touch on themes later to be elaborated, but when the reader comes to the one sketch among the lot set not in New Orleans but in a rural venue, he suddenly feels that Faulkner had perhaps unwittingly found one of the directions in which his work should go. "The Liar," as Carvel Collins remarked, unearthing these *New Orleans Sketches* in 1958, is the first of Faulkner's writings to present a teller of tall tales.[1] Collins noted that the country store in which "The Liar" is set would in time become Will Varner's store in *The Hamlet*, and that the sketch contains another motif elaborated in that novel, a horse running through a house. There is also a character named Ek—the odd name reappears as Eck Snopes in the same novel. Another germ of a future fiction in "The Liar" is the country folk who have never seen a railroad, prefiguring Ringo in *The Unvanquished*.

Faulkner wrote "The Liar" not in New Orleans but on shipboard, en route to Europe. It is as though while living in the Vieux Carré he could scarcely resist attempting to record the

1. Carvel Collins, Introduction to William Faulkner, *New Orleans Sketches* (New Brunswick, 1958), 27, 31.

1

cosmopolitan characters and the variegated life around him, seemingly so much richer in personalities and incidents than anything remembered from his youth in a small and sleepy Mississippi town. It was not until he had separated himself from these inviting scenes that his imagination could search memory for a different setting, for the rhythms and tones not of contemporary city life but of folktale. New Orleans would continue to figure in his fiction, but only tangentially, for it is far beyond the borders of Faulkner's invented rural county, Yoknapatawpha. With its French traditions, its Cajuns and Creoles, its Spanish tinge, and the imprint of its Caribbean contacts, New Orleans has the appearance of a European capital mysteriously decaying in the tropics. It is from New Orleans that Thomas Sutpen inexplicably emerges, in *Absalom, Absalom!*, bringing to Mississippi his captive French architect and twenty Negro slaves. It is there that Charles Bon keeps his octoroon mistress in *fin de siècle* elegance, there that Henry Sutpen is introduced to a libertinism unknown up-country.

Contemporary New Orleans is the setting for two of Faulkner's minor novels. In *Mosquitoes* (1927), an expansion of the milieu of "Chartres Street," the city is the home of sophisticates and would-be sophisticates. In *Pylon* (1935), a novel about the hopeless lives of barnstorming aviators, New Valois (New Orleans) is an extended image of the contemporary Waste Land. But the country setting explored in "The Liar" summons up characters and motifs that must have resonated in Faulkner's imagination, for they recur, greatly elaborated and perfected, in his late novels.

In "The Liar," four men are lounging on the porch of Gibson's store. One of them, Ek, takes some ribbing from the rest for telling lies. A stranger appears, and silently munches his cheese and crackers while Ek launches a tale he swears is true: how the sheriff, needing a hill man to intercede with some folks he had to interview, had driven Ek away up into the hills. Then on foot they had approached a hardscrabble farm, the sheriff and his deputy going one way, Ek the other. Alone, Ek then witnessed a rendezvous between a woman carrying a carpetbag and a man down by the spring. A second man arrived, who brained the first with a fence rail and dropped his body down a dry well. This is told in country idiom—"There I was, watching murder, skeered to move, and no sign of sheriff and Tim. I've got along fine without law officers, but I sho needed one of them. . . . I was past thinking; jest goggle-eyed, like a fish when you jerk him out the water." Ek feels a sudden chill in the air and doesn't want to continue; and as he does, the stranger suddenly pulls a pistol, shoots him, and dashes down to the tracks to board a moving train.

Later, when the doctor had ridden ten miles, dressed Ek's shoulder, cursed him for a fool, and gone, the four of them took him to task.

"Well, Ek, I guess you learnt your lesson. You'll know better than tell the truth again. . . .

Ek turned his fever exasperated face to them. "I tell you that it was all a lie, ever last word of it. . . ." And convicted of both truthfulness and stupidity, he turned his face bitterly to the wall, knowing that his veracity as a liar was gone forever.[2]

The dynamics of this little tale are perhaps more complex than at first appears. Ek's companions, who know him as a "liar," take at face value his announcing that his tale is true, even though in establishing his *bona fides* as a hill man he tells them he had never worn shoes until his twenty-first birthday, and "when they come to my pallet that morning with them new shoes, I up and lit out of there in my shirt tail and took to the woods. Paw sent word around to the neighbors and they organized a hunt same as a bear hunt, with axes and ropes and dogs. No guns, though. . . . [I]t took 'em two days to git me." This manhunt, prefiguring Uncle Buck McCaslin's pursuit of Tomey's Turl in the opening tale in *Go Down, Moses*, is surely a send-up, but Ek's auditors accept it as truth without demur. Thus a lie looks like truth; indeed, the whole yarn of the witnessed murder, an outright fabrication, proves to have described an actual murder in such accurate detail that the liar is nearly murdered himself by the guilty stranger. "If you were lying," Gibson tells

2. Faulkner, *New Orleans Sketches*, 171–85.

him, "you ought to be shot for telling one so prob'le that it reely happened somewhere."[3] "The Liar" is a fable about the imaginative power—and danger—of the tale-teller.

By this time Faulkner was already the author of many sketches, stories, reviews, and poems, and was the artist whose Beardsleyesque cartoons had appeared in student publications at the University of Mississippi.[4] These apprentice pieces reveal the early influences to which Faulkner responded and help us trace the emergence of his mature talent. As Thomas McHaney perceptively remarks, a young writer must be different from those around him, and what could be more different from his fellow students at Ole Miss than an R.A.F. veteran imbued with the languors of French symbolist poetry and the world-weary attitudes of the Decadence of the English Nineties?[5] A case has been made by Judith Sensibar for the permanent formative effect upon Faulkner's successes in fiction of his attempts in these early years to be a poet, but although he kept in his repertoire of styles elements learned from Mallarmé, Swinburne, and the early Yeats, it is hard to believe that his failed poetry, derivative in style and lacking verbal intensity, contains the principal germ of his power as a novelist. McHaney is more on the mark in noting the many resources upon which Faulkner drew, "absorbing Conrad, Eliot, Freud, Frazer, Bergson, Einstein, Joyce, Jung, Anderson, Cezanne, Picasso, and Matisse"—these the influences through which, McHaney says, "the tall tale style of people like Ratliff [was] inherited."[6] It's a rich mixture, all right, but in attending to these more sophisticated sources from literature, science, psychology, and art, let us not lose sight of the archetypes, rhythms, and style of the oral folktale, which of course Faulkner

3. *Ibid.*

4. Carvel Collins (ed.), *William Faulkner: Early Prose and Poetry* (Boston, 1962).

5. Thomas L. McHaney, "What Faulkner Learned from the Tall Tale," in Doreen Fowler and Ann J. Abadie (eds.), *Faulkner and Humor* (Jackson, Miss., 1986), 110–36.

6. Judith L. Sensibar, *The Origins of Faulkner's Art* (Austin, 1984); McHaney, "What Faulkner Learned," 116.

used for more complex purposes than the original tellers of the yarns he borrowed, stole, and almost always transformed, could have imagined.

In the first ten years or so of his attempts to be an author, living in rural Mississippi with folklore to be heard all around him, Faulkner took no heed of its possibilities. Indeed, precisely because it was too close by, was an integral part of the real life from which at this early stage he felt he must differentiate himself, he had to ignore it. In a note on Eugene O'Neill in 1922, he gratuitously states that "a national literature cannot spring from folk lore—though heaven knows, such a forcing has been tried often enough—for America is too big and there are too many folk lores." Instead, Faulkner writes, the "earthy strength" of American spoken English will nourish our literature.[7] In his own quest for that idiomatic strength, Faulkner soon came to imagine its earthy speakers and what they spoke, although of course such a stylistic development reflects an expansion of theme as well as of language.

In 1926 Faulkner wrote an extended sketch of some twenty thousand words which, despite repeated efforts to expand and revise it, he was unable to complete until 1940. This piece, *Father Abraham*, unpublished until 1983, reads like an almost-finished draft for parts of *The Hamlet*, chronicling Flem Snopes's marriage to the pregnant Eula Varner, the sudden departure of her suitors, Flem's return from Texas with a string of ponies, and the auction of these spotted horses. Here, introduced incipiently but scarcely developed, is the contrast between the carnival of human greed, lust, and sorrow, and the imperturbability of nature. At dawn "the mockingbird returned to the appletree across the way and sang," the apple tree to become, fifteen years later, a flowering pear, a leitmotif in Faulkner's fugue of styles in *The Hamlet*, in which the rough timbres and vivid imagery of folk speech are counterpoised to refulgent diction derived from his

7. Collins (ed.), *Early Prose and Poetry*, 89. Faulkner's uses of country speech are detailed by Calvin S. Brown in *A Glossary of Faulkner's South* (New Haven, 1976).

poetic period.[8] It was in *Father Abraham*, then, in 1926, that Faulkner, responding to Sherwood Anderson's advice, "discovered that my own little postage stamp of native soil was worth writing about and I would never live long enough to exhaust it."[9] What he found there, among the redneck tribe of Snopeses, was the form, the substance, and the style of the American folk story, the tall tale. In the persona of his sewing-machine agent (called V. K. Suratt in *Father Abraham*, V. K. Ratliff in *The Hamlet*), he adopted the tone of voice of the narrator traditional in American folk humor.

In his sketch "How to Tell a Story," Mark Twain has set down for posterity the proper American tone in the comic monologue: not striving for wit, as do the French, nor producing a punch line, as do the English, but providing a deadpan accumulation of one irrelevancy or piece of preposterousness after another with nary the downcracking of a smile. After "The Liar," we find Faulkner next trying this mode in a scene in *Mosquitoes* in which the novelist Dawson Fairchild tries, with some success, to gull a visiting Englishman. A yarn, casually introduced, about one Al Jackson, descended from "Old Hickory that licked you folks in 1812," who wears congress boots while bathing to conceal his "family deformity" on which account Old Hickory fought the Battle of New Orleans in the swamps where his webbed feet were an advantage, segues into still greater absurdities. General Jackson had a farm in Florida where his Tennessee horse "strayed off into the swamps, and in someway the breed got crossed with alligators"; in the Battle of New Orleans, Old Hickory mounted his infantry on those half-horse half-alligators, "and the British couldn't stop 'em at all."[10]

Fairchild, the straight-faced leg-puller, is Faulkner's portrait

8. William Faulkner, *Father Abraham* (New York, 1984), 30. This first trade edition was preceded by a limited edition (New York, 1983).

9. Faulkner, interview by Jean Stein vanden Heuvel (*Paris Review*, 1956), rpr. in James B. Meriwether and Michael Millgate (eds.), *Lion in the Garden: Interviews with William Faulkner, 1926–62* (New York, 1968), 255.

10. "How to Tell a Story," in *Literary Essays* (New York, 1899), 8–15; William Faulkner, *Mosquitoes* (New York, 1927), 66, 67, 68.

of his New Orleans friend Sherwood Anderson, and indeed the Al Jackson yarns in *Mosquitoes* are a reprise of a joking tall-tale correspondence between the older writer and his protégé. There is in their letters much elaboration of Jackson's genealogy, his fish farm, the transformation of one of the Jacksons into a shark who bothers fat blonde swimmers. That this somewhat labored jocosity has literary as well as folktale roots appears in the fate of another Jackson, as Faulkner describes it:

Old man Jackson didn't believe in education. But the boy Herman was crazy to learn to read. . . . At last, at the age of eighteen, he learned . . . and he established a record. He read Sir Walter Scott's complete works in twelve and one half days. For two days afterward he seemed to be dazed—could not remember who he was. So a schoolmate wrote his name on a card which Herman carried in his hand. . . .

Then on the third day he went into convulsions . . . dying after days of terrible agony.[11]

Herman's fate is reminiscent of that of the boy Mark Twain describes in *Life on the Mississippi* who was reduced to idiocy after memorizing the entire Bible for Sunday School. In the same book Mark Twain makes Sir Walter responsible for the Civil War by his incitement of the South to adopt the ways of medieval chivalry. Incipient in Faulkner's yarn is the contrast between the two strains of Mississippi narrative his later fiction would explore: the Sir Walter Scott strain in his examination of the chivalric code of such aristocrats as Colonel Sartoris in *Flags in the Dust* and *The Unvanquished*, the Al Jackson strain in Ratliff's deadpan yarning and the preposterousness of incident in the trickster tales and the horse auction of *The Hamlet*, which, as we shall see, have other proximate sources in folktale and in popular literature as well.

The leg-pulls in *Mosquitoes* are of a cruder sort than appear in Faulkner's later fictions. These whoppers, however, resemble others that Faulkner launched in real life, such as lying his way

11. Faulkner, *Mosquitoes*, 86–88. Faulkner's Jackson letters to Anderson are printed as "Al Jackson" in Joseph Blotner (ed.), *Uncollected Stories of William Faulkner* (New York, 1979), 474–79.

into the R.A.F. in Canada, returning to Mississippi with feigned combat experience and wounds, telling newspaper interviewers windies about his descent from a Negro slave and an alligator, and pretending to be a simple farmer unacquainted with literary people. Faulkner relished playing many roles, and he drew on oral folk humor for some of them which he opposed, in life, as in his writing, with such other roles as the lovesick poet or the country gentleman riding to hounds.

Robert Penn Warren was doubtless right when he wrote that Faulkner probably derived his strain of frontier humor "from the porches of country stores and the courthouse yards of county-seat towns and not from any book," yet he is known to have read in and borrowed from the work of several Southern humorists. One, Augustus Baldwin Longstreet, was the first president of the University of Mississippi and is buried in the same graveyard as Faulkner and his family. Longstreet's *Georgia Scenes* (1835) was praised by Poe for its humor, its "exquisitely discriminative and penetrating understanding . . . of Southern character," the wit shown in "The Horse-Swap," and the "dramatic vigor" with which scenes of "barbarity" are portrayed. Longstreet's sketches enclose the rough-and-tumble comedy of local mores within the frame of commentary by the visiting gentleman who narrates the tales. Longstreet's Ransy Sniffle is "a misshapen urchin . . . all the pleasures of whose life concentre on a love of fisticuffs," and is a probable model for Faulkner's Snopeses.[12]

It has been proposed that *As I Lay Dying* derives from a sketch, "Well, Dad's Dead!" by George Washington Harris, but this seems unlikely since the sketch was not included in Harris' *Sut Lovingood: Yarns Spun by a "Nat'ral Born Durn'd Fool"* (1867) but languished in a Knoxville newspaper until discovered by a contemporary scholar.[13] No doubt there was, and perhaps

12. Robert Penn Warren, "William Faulkner," in Frederick J. Hoffman and Olga W. Vickery (eds.), *William Faulkner: Three Decades of Criticism* (East Lansing, 1960), 118; Edgar Allan Poe, *Complete Works*, ed. James A. Harrison (17 vols.; New York, 1902), VIII, 257–65.

13. Thomas Inge, "Faulkner and George Washington Harris: In the Tradition of Southwestern Humor," *Tennessee Studies in Literature*, VII (1962), 47–59.

still is, an oral tradition of stories about outrageous funerals, but this is not the sort of yarn folks tell to strangers with notebooks or tape recorders.[14] *As I Lay Dying* clearly shares attributes of folk humor; the lack of a detectable source, however, points to the comment of Robert Penn Warren's quoted above, that Faulkner absorbed such material more likely from oral tradition than from books.

Yet it is indubitable that he absorbed something from *Sut Lovingood*, a volume he owned. As Thomas Inge has noted, the stampede of wild horses in *The Hamlet* may be based on Sut Lovingood's turning loose among the quilts on a clothesline "a hoss, a wild, skeery, wall-eyed devil," then hitting the horse with a fence paling so that it runs wildly through the quilts and causes the death of Mrs. Yardley. Edmund Wilson has called *Sut Lovingood* "by far the most repellent book of any real literary merit in American literature," finding Sut "a peasant squatting in his own filth . . . avenging his inferiority by tormenting other people. His impulse is avowedly sadistic."[15] Sut, a bottom dog, revels in cruel practical jokes, in revenges. He is obviously a rough draft of Faulkner's treatment of the Snopeses, and his yarns read as though Mink Snopes had been gifted with vivid metaphor.

The real influence of *Sut Lovingood* on Faulkner was not so

14. In my search of folktales collected by members of the Mississippi Federal Writers Project during the 1930s (files in Jackson and the Library of Congress), I found not one allusion to such absurd or outrageous funeral practices as provide the plot for *As I Lay Dying*. This omission is not surprising; informants would withhold such unseemly yarns, the telling of which would reflect adversely on their own status. Further, if any such were told, the collectors would suppress them from files to be considered for publication in the state guidebook. It is only in very recent years that folklore scholarship, responding to the loosening of outlook in the general culture, has considered materials hitherto inadmissible. Vance Randolph, the doyen of Ozark folklore collectors, published during the 1940s and 1950s six volumes of tales and songs, but his stock of sexually explicit yarns, *Pissing in the Snow*, could not appear until 1976.

15. Inge, "Faulkner and George Washington Harris," 50; Edmund Wilson, *Patriotic Gore: Studies in the Literature of the American Civil War* (New York, 1962), 509–10, 516.

much the plot of the horse stampede as its being the first literary treatment of the poor white as seen from the inside (without Longstreet's condescension) but with all his resentments and what Wilson calls his "ferocious fantasies." In these, as well as in his pacific passages, there is what F. O. Matthiessen calls "a wonderfully kinetic quality," likening Harris' comic gift to Melville's tragic, a "rare kind of dramatic imagination."[16] Written in orthographic dialect, *Sut* makes for hard reading these days; but a translation into standard English, published in 1954, virtually extinguished *Sut's* vivid, angry fire. *Sut Lovingood* remains a minor masterpiece, the literary expression of the downtrodden, resentful, and resilient cracker. Faulkner, whose gift is as much greater than Harris' as his vision of human fate is broader, draws on Harris' book and on the traditions of speech and feeling it expresses to forge his own stylistic *tours de force* in *The Hamlet* and his other novels and stories.

Harris and Longstreet are but two of the written sources for this vein in Faulkner's work. There is of course Mark Twain, and Johnson Jones Hooper, whose *Adventures of Captain Simon Suggs* provided Twain with the camp meeting scene in *Huckleberry Finn*. What Faulkner borrowed from, or shares with, these writers is his capturing the cadence and syntax of country speech. Not only the humor of the folktale, adapted in the wry bantering tone of Ratliff and the rough comic exaggerations of Uncle Buck McCaslin, but the very form and movement of Faulkner's famous involuted style derive at least in part from the rhythms of telling. In the oral recitation, as Mark Twain defined and practiced it, the point of the tale is purposefully delayed by the introduction of seemingly random divigations, as in Jim Baker's tale of his grandfather's ram (in *Roughing It*); the detours and byways, in Faulkner, may indeed be more to the point than is the putative point of the story.

This technique of the wayward narrator, employing the syntax, speech, rhythms, and vocabulary appropriate to the character of the speaker, was used by Mark Twain primarily for comic

16. F. O. Matthiessen, *American Renaissance* (New York, 1941), 644.

ends but in Faulkner's hands becomes a flexible instrument indeed. The whole of *Absalom, Absalom!* is a told narration, in which one teller tells what another teller told him; sometimes the narrative we are given is repeated at third hand, as when Quentin tells Shreve what Mr. Compson had repeated to him of what Rosa Coldfield had said. Thus is the truth about Thomas Sutpen enwrapped, ensnared, entangled in memories of memory, in the ways one character's character at the same time conserves and distorts what another had said. This technique, which Faulkner may have learned in part from Conrad, seems a far piece from folktale, but it is essentially similar to the way in which Ratliff's point of view determines what we learn and how we learn it in *The Hamlet,* and to the effect of a displaced narrator in "Was" (*Go Down, Moses*), which makes possible Isaac McCaslin's retelling what Cass Edmonds told him that Cass, when nine years old, had witnessed and taken part in, before Isaac was born.

Thus the delaying tactics of the comic folktale are similar to and may be among the sources of what Conrad Aiken described in 1939 as Faulkner's "whole elaborate method of *deliberately withheld meaning,* of progressive and delayed disclosure, which so often gives the characteristic shape to the novels themselves."[17] The justification for this withholding, for the partial revelations, is to create a text that will replicate in the experience of the reader the experience of the character in all its complexity and confusion, so that the truth of the matter, when put together at last from the fragmentary evidence and finally grasped, will be no mere oversimplification but a fairly felt participation in the gradual process of its discovery.

Surveying the first dozen years of Faulkner's career, one is struck by the way he seemed mired in aestheticism, struggling with little development to write poetic imitations of Verlaine, adopting the mannerisms of the French symbolists and diction bor-

17. Conrad Aiken, "William Faulkner: The Novel as Form," in Linda Welshimer Wagner (ed.), *William Faulkner: Four Decades of Criticism* (East Lansing, 1973), 136.

rowed without modification from Swinburne, early Yeats, the Eliot of "Prufrock." His poems use such conventional figures as Pierrot and Columbine, nymphs and fauns. The chief contribution of his limp, imitative verse to his later fiction, besides a tendency to indulge in decadent diction, is the use of an imagined persona, the conventional Pierrot, as a way of projecting his feelings. Although writing after the appearance of Pound's early poems and *The Waste Land*, *Harmonium*, and *Spring and All*, the young poet in Mississippi seems quite untouched by the great shift in sensibility announced by these early modernist works. As late as April, 1925, he wrote, in an article entitled "Verse Old and Nascent: A Pilgrimage," of his admiration for Swinburne, Robinson, Frost, Aiken, and especially Housman, concluding, "Is not there among us someone who can write something beautiful and passionate and sad instead of saddening?"[18] It is as though his taste had scarcely moved beyond that of the Decadents of the turn of the century. His own verse is purpureal, languid, as lacking in energy as in originality.

In prose, however, the young writer was not so circumscribed. He could, it is true, write (in *Mayday*, 1926), an allegorical, artificial diction more suggestive of James Branch Cabell than of the Arthurian romances he thought he was emulating. But his Chartres Street sketches are in a style altogether different from this poetic prose, as they differ from his poems. Journalistic, descriptive, their diction and syntax are serviceable though undistinguished. By 1926, however, he had already drafted two longer works, neither published until much later, which break powerfully free from the insipidities of the aforementioned apprentice works. *Father Abraham* and *Flags in the Dust* (a truncated version of which was published as *Sartoris* in 1929, the full text not until 1973) sketched out the contours of Faulkner's imaginative vision of Yoknapatawpha, his invented county, in terms of the interlocked histories of several clans—Sartorises, McCaslins, Snopeses—and revealed the development of his mature styles. *Flags in the Dust* is written with an intensity and

18. Collins (ed.), *Early Prose and Poetry*, 114–18.

lyricism that suggest not the hand-me-down verse conventions of his poems but the vivifying influences of Conrad and Melville, while *Father Abraham*, as we have seen, opens up the territory of colloquial language and syntax, the narrative rhythms of the oral tradition.

For his imagination freely to explore and embody his deepest feelings, Faulkner needed to put between himself and his writing the perspective and distance made possible by his animating fictive characters. His self speaking in poems as the self—even when displaced as Pierrot—has only one voice, can deal only with its own blighted hopes, its own wounds. But the self split among a whole cast of persons, its constituent parts, can speak through each of them, finding for each a manner of speech appropriate to its role and character. In *Flags in the Dust*, Faulkner splits the self between its active and its passive roles. Horace Benbow represents the dreamy, idealistic, poetic side of the self, incapable of effective action, dangerously drawn to an incestuous attachment to his sister Narcissa. The active self is split again into halves as the Sartoris twins, grandsons of the aged Bayard Sartoris (who would be the young hero of the as-yet-unwritten *The Unvanquished*). The twins are both aviators in World War I; John, named for his great-grandfather, the dashing Civil War colonel in *The Unvanquished*, is killed in a needless, reckless dogfight, witnessed by his brother Bayard, who is unable to save him and so returns home with the unappeasable guilt of being a survivor as well as with the Sartoris penchant for self-destruction. Bayard Sartoris carries into the twentieth century the baggage of his Civil War ancestor's code, his recklessness, his inadaptability. These qualities are highlighted by Faulkner's contrasting with Bayard another character embodying the active spirit: Buddy McCallum is a simpler, more innocent man, living with his father and tribe of brothers in the deep woods in a sort of primitive hunting society, untouched by the spiritual anguish of the aristocrat alienated from his time.

The way opens toward the embodiment in fiction of persons still more diverse, of language and syntax more varied still. Style serves to embody the consciousness of the narrator or the character, not the author; and if the narrator feels and thinks in a sentence five pages long, as will Ike McCaslin in "The Bear," we accept this syntactical entanglement because the force of Isaac's character compels us to do so. Where Faulkner fails stylistically is in the attribution of a level of diction inappropriate to the character who says or thinks it. Thus the stream of consciousness style that works so well for Isaac McCaslin seems foisted upon fourteen-year-old Chick Mallison, who narrates *Intruder in the Dust.* We are not made to feel that the five-page sentences and involuted associations given here are in fact the way this character's mind apprehends his experiences; rather, we feel these as the willed impositions of authorial techniques. Usually, the points at which a character speaks out of character are those where Faulkner adopts a language "poetic" in the pejorative sense, a recrudescence of his own persona as a failed poet.

It is truly remarkable how *Father Abraham* and *Flags in the Dust* between them contain the seeds of Faulkner's entire ouevre, the history of Yoknapatawpha County. Characters, conflicts, relationships, plots, short stories, whole novels will exfoliate from these early texts. Even in them, although the effect is diffused, Faulkner interprets character in terms of family history and family history in terms of character. As the vivid persons he had created assumed, in his imagination, lives of their own, each contemporary character presented himself as the inheritor of a history waiting to be explored. Most of Faulkner's novels are chronicle-histories of one or another family. In *Flags in the Dust* he identified the Sartoris family with the aristocratic class and its loss of relevance and power. Although the Sartoris virtues no longer embody the ethos of a dominant class or meet the needs of society, they linger in the querulousness of an old man and in the irresponsible gestures of a youth with neither hope nor a role in his society. And in *Father Abraham* Faulkner begins the adventures of another family, another class: the tribe of Snopeses who would overrun Yoknapatawpha County with their calculating greed, selfishness, and lack of human feeling.

In his concentration upon his "little postage stamp of earth," Faulkner brings to its highest intensity the hitherto desultory impulses of the local color movement, merging its depiction of the singularities of life and language in a particular region with the larger design of the dynastic novel. The American fiction writer has on the whole had to struggle against the restrictions of his subject matter, life in the United States, the limitations of which Henry James so tellingly itemized in his discussion of the paucity of incident in Hawthorne's *American Notebooks*. But unlike Hawthorne's bleakly egalitarian New England, the Southern life Faulkner beheld was more like the French or English situations James regarded as optimal, at least resembling those in its stratified class system, its gallery of character types ranging from poor white trash, horse traders, gamblers, and sturdy white yeomen to storekeepers, lawyers, bankers, outsized Confederate colonels, and a gamut of Negro characters in various degrees of servitude and independence. In the range of his interlocked chronicles of the several dynasties in Yoknapatawpha County, Faulkner resembles his proximate model, Balzac, as well as Hardy and Arnold Bennett.[19] No other American novelist approaches Faulkner in the success and magnitude of such a grand fictional design. In the enactment of that design in his novels, archetypes from myth intersect with history as well as with the plots, characters, style, and narrative methods Faulkner borrowed or adapted from folklore.

HISTORY AS MYTH, MYTH AS HISTORY

In the empirical structures of his novels, as in his uses of motifs, characters, and conflicts from native folklore and from myth,

19. Faulkner read Balzac among his grandfather's books; Balzac was especially valued by Faulkner's mentor, Phil Stone, and influenced Faulkner's conception of the Snopes novels, to the first of which, *The Hamlet*, he originally gave the Balzacian title "The Peasants" (Joseph Blotner, *Faulkner: A Biography* [2 vols.; New York, 1974], I, 160, 192, 299, 537, II, 960). At the University of Virginia, Faulkner said he read "some Balzac almost every year," and he referred to Balzac and Dickens as having "a concept of a cosmos in miniature" (Frederick L. Gwynn and Joseph L. Blotner [eds.], *Faulkner in the University* [New York, 1959], 50, 232).

Faulkner is truly in the American grain. He carries on into the twentieth century the experimental and experiential struggles to create new fictional forms commensurate with the contingent nature of truth that characterized the best works of Hawthorne, Melville, and Mark Twain. Allied with Joyce and Conrad in his modernism, Faulkner is at the same time in the line of these American forebears. He shares not only their improvised narrative forms (as in *The House of the Seven Gables* and *The Blithedale Romance, Moby-Dick* and *The Confidence-Man, The Adventures of Huckleberry Finn* and *Pudd'nhead Wilson*) but also their receptivity to the traditional materials of myth and literary expressions of the folk imagination in the exploration of his themes.

Yet it is hard to think of an author whose imagination is as deeply implicated in historical fact, or the appearance of fact, as is Faulkner's. Each person in Yoknapatawpha is the sum of the train of events, relationships, acts, and feelings that make up his being. Even things have their stories, which is to say their histories, whether already achieved or imagined before the occurrence of the facts. For instance, in *The Hamlet*, the voluptuous Eula Varner is courted by three country youths whose "fairly well-horsed buggies stood in steady rotation along a picket fence," but now that the pregnant Eula has been married off by her father to Flem Snopes and is about to leave on the Texas train, Ratliff, sorrowfully observing her departure, observes also the abandoned buggy of one of her unsuccessful suitors who has decamped in haste.

Ratliff was to see it, discovered a few months afterward, standing empty and with propped shafts in a stable shed a few miles from the village, gathering dust; chickens roosted upon it, steadily streaking and marring the once-bright varnish with limelike droppings, until the next harvest, the money-time, when the father of its late driver sold it to a Negro farmhand, after which it would be seen passing through the village a few times each year, perhaps recognised, perhaps not, while its new owner married and began to get a family and then turn gray, spilling children, no longer glittering, its wheels wired upright in succession by crossed barrel staves until staves and delicate wheels both vanished, translated apparently in motion at some point into stout, not new, slightly smaller wagon wheels, giving it a list, the list too interchangeable, ranging from quarter to quarter between two of its passing appearances behind a succession of spavined and bony horses and mules in wire- and rope-patched harness, as if its owner had horsed it ten minutes ago out of a secret boneyard for this particular final swansong's apotheosis which, woefully misinformed as to its own capacities, was each time not the last.[20]

Such specificity, such a concentration upon the interaction of time with things, would seem the opposite of the mythic imagination, which subsumes all actions under the patterns of the archetypes they embody. The chronicle of the suitor's wagon, writ large, comprises the composite stories, hence the history, of Yoknapatawpha County. But story becoming history, if it is to transcend the unending recital of random, disconnected, meaningless events, must participate in a discernible pattern, an inherent action larger and grander than the quotidian details of its telling. As Faulkner writes, in *A Fable*, of an interpolated folktale about a stolen three-legged racehorse, "being immortal, the story, the legend, was not to be owned by any of one of the pairs [of characters] who added to its shining and tragic increment, but only to be used, passed through, by each in their doomed and homeless turn."[21]

The relationship between historical data and the transcendent and legendary meanings that inhere in them has been addressed by Nicholas Berdyaev in terms appropriate to Faulkner's imagination. "History," says Berdyaev, "is not an objective empirical datum; it is a myth." Believing that each man contains within his inner nature "a sort of microcosm in which the whole world of reality and all the great historical epochs combine and coexist," the Russian philosopher posits the individual consciousness as a sensorium of historical knowledge; and that knowledge proves to be "immortal, the story, the legend."

20. Faulkner, *The Hamlet* (1940; rpr. New York, 1956), 147, 148.
21. Faulkner, *A Fable* (New York, 1978), 129.

Myth is no fiction, but a reality. . . . Historical myths have a profound significance for the act of remembrance. A myth contains the story that is preserved in popular memory and that helps to bring to life some deep stratum buried in the depths of human spirit. . . . [T]he significance of the part played by tradition in the inner comprehension of history [is that it] makes possible a great and occult act of remembrance. It represents, indeed, no external impulse or externally imposed fact alien to man, but one that is a manifestation of the inner mysteriousness of life, in which he can attain to knowledge and feel himself to be an inalienable participant.[22]

This is to say that a nation's history comprises the received and inborn pattern of knowledge with which its citizens are endowed and in which, knowingly or otherwise, they participate. The culturally received patterns of experience available to the American writer include the remembrance of national history, the Judeo-Christian tradition, the pagan past of classical and primitive myth, and the rambunctious annals of native folklore. From the beginnings of American settlement it was felt that colonial life reenacted the Bible. Governor Bradford's *Journal* and the writings of other Puritan and Quaker worthies abundantly show that the first settlers saw themselves as reliving the annals of the Israelites seeking the Promised Land in a wilderness, or else attempting to experience once again the primal innocence of an Edenic life in a new world free from the corruptions of European civilization. Inescapably bringing with them the intellectual baggage of the Europe from which they would free themselves, Americans celebrated their heroes and the fertility of their new continent in terms borrowed from Homer, Virgil, and Ovid. In time a folk thesaurus developed here of new legendry, or of inherited tales remade. Regional characters emerged as recognizable types, the Yankee and the frontiersman, cast in innumerable conflicts. Natural and human fecundity were celebrated in folk comedy and in supernaturalism free of Christian restraint, while the evil sides of man and of nature were expressed in the folklore of demonism and witchcraft. A bump-

22. Nicholas Berdyaev, *The Meaning of History* (1923), trans. George Reavey (New York, 1936), 21, 22, 23–24.

tious lexicon of folk speech enriched the American language. Thus in character, sketch, tall tale, jokelore, superstition, and folk speech, a cast of characters, rudimentary plots, and metaphors explored the natural and supernatural world.

The tone of this American folklore was ebullient, self-confident, comic. The American, as revealed in this lore, was adaptable to circumstance, undaunted by adversity, at any moment ready to change his calling, be born into a new identity, go west and grow up with the country. Reflecting a new society in which status was achieved, not ascribed by rigid and inherited class lines, the transformations of the metamorphic hero dramatized the hope of upward mobility while blithely ignoring the costs in human relationships of such alienations from one's beginnings. At the same time, in antebellum popular literature there emerged fictional figures who expressed the negative, irresponsible aspects of the metamorphic man, as seen in Thomas Chandler Haliburton's Sam Slick and Hooper's Simon Suggs. As I have shown in *Form and Fable in American Fiction*, the literary combination of these properties, both inherited and natively grown, prefigured in Washington Irving's stories "Rip Van Winkle" and "The Legend of Sleepy Hollow," was embodied in the romances of Hawthorne, Melville, and Mark Twain. In them we find the optimism of the metamorphic hero—Holgrave, Ishmael, Huck Finn—and also the negative implications of metamorphosis; these include fraudulence (for when a man has so many identities, which is the real person?), allied with demonism in Hawthorne's Dr. Westerveldt and Melville's Confidence-Man, and parodically, with the illusions of the artist in Tom Sawyer, the Duke, and the Dauphin.[23] Faulkner's work brings into mid–twentieth century these conventions, these mythical and folk archetypes. Yet, as is always true of him, he transformed what he borrowed or adapted.

For the nineteenth-century romancers, America represented the promises, whether delivered or betrayed by experience, of freedom, of life under unprecedented political arrangements;

23. *Form and Fable in American Fiction* (New York, 1961).

whereas Europe embodied feudalism, oppression, suffering, defeat. American life was innocence, Europe was a past burdened with guilt, as its history, myths, and superstitions attested. Faulkner, however, had no need to turn to Europe and its past for images of tragedy or defeat, for these were the fate of the South after the Civil War. Unlike the rest of the United States, Faulkner's region—even his home town—had known the invasion of alien armies, skirmishes and battles, destruction of homes, looting of property, the death of its young men, and, after the war, the long, difficult effort to reconstitute a society rent apart by defeat, pillage, and devastation.

The Old South differed from the rest of the United States also in that its inflexibly hierarchical social system made mobility between the classes much less feasible than elsewhere. The egalitarianism to which, at least in principle, the institutions, rhetoric, and folk fantasies of American public life in other regions were committed was, in the South, greatly compromised by a social system based upon chattel slavery. These were the social conditions that Mark Twain had represented in medieval costume in *A Connecticut Yankee in King Arthur's Court*, a book in which the simple application of egalitarian Yankee pragmatism to a feudal slavocracy led not to a more just society but to revolt and holocaust. The intransigence of the South to the democratic dogma espoused elsewhere in the United States is what most characterized the culture and history of that region. In effect, in Faulkner's donnée, the values attributed to Europe by his authorial forebears were characteristic of Southern history and were internalized in the experiences of Southern men and women aware of their own heritage, as Berdyaev had said was true for Europeans.

Thus the South had developed its own attitudes to its own historical experience, assumptions Faulkner shared and developed further in his fiction while criticizing them at the same time. Among many commentators on this theme Lewis P. Simpson has explored it most deeply, showing how Faulkner was anticipated by the antebellum Southern writers in their need to defend the peculiar institutions that composed an intrinsic part of the pastoral society they regarded as an earthly paradise, and how, after the war, the literary memory of slavery times was inevitably tinged by the presence of the central cause of the tragedy of the Fall of the South. This view in truth comprises a "myth" of Southern history, a secularization of the biblical theme of the Garden of Eden and the inescapable presence therein of original sin.[24] The tension is strong, in Faulkner's work, between the desire to have had a prelapsarian history and the realization that even before the war the seed was sown of the defeat of the South, the destruction of its way of life, and the downfall of its aristocracy.

Like Hawthorne, Poe, Melville, and Mark Twain before him, Faulkner savored imagining himself a disinherited aristocrat. In varying degrees and ways, our nineteenth-century writers made use of this theme—the obverse of the upward social mobility represented by the metamorphic hero—which the circumstances of their family histories, as they perceived them, thrust into their fictions. In works as different from one another as *The House of the Seven Gables*, "The Fall of the House of Usher," *Pierre, The American Claimant*, and *Pudd'nhead Wilson*, whether in satire or in sorrow at their exile from man's kingly estate in the Garden, theirs was a sense of loss and diminution in the world, deprivations of rank, possessions, and grace. The disinherited aristocrat experienced in his personal and family history a retelling of the Fall of Man. At the same time, except for the Southerner Poe, these authors were committed to the democratic spirit of the country and the age. Its levelling egalitarianism was in conflict with the vestigial aristocratic memories or hopes each could not refrain from projecting onto his characters.

Thus like his own forebears, Hawthorne's Pyncheons seek,

24. Lewis P. Simpson, *The Man of Letters in New England and the South: Essays on the History of the Literary Vocation in America* (Baton Rouge, 1973), 167–91; *The Dispossessed Garden: Pastoral and History in Southern Literature* (Athens, Ga., 1975); "Yoknapatawpha and Faulkner's Fable of Civilization," in Evans Harrington and Ann J. Abadie (eds.), *The Maker and the Myth: Faulkner and Yoknapatawpha* (Jackson, Miss., 1978); *The Brazen Face of History: Studies in the Literary Consciousness in America* (Baton Rouge, 1980).

while his Holgrave derides, their lost deed that would confer title to an earldom in Maine. Poe, who actually was disinherited by the wealthy (though not aristocratic) Richmond merchant who had reared him, and Melville, descended from heroic Revolutionary generals to witness his father's bankruptcy and madness, made of these losses metaphoric actions in their fictions. So too did Mark Twain, whose father's failed law practice and general store on the Missouri frontier seemed a bitter comedown for a Virginia gentleman with a claim to vast lands in Tennessee.

Faulkner, too, was descended from a proud and distinguished ancestor whose present seed had come somewhat down in the world. His great-grandfather, W. C. Falkner, was a swashbuckling Confederate colonel with, it is true, a somewhat equivocal record of military achievements, but around whom an aura of heroic legend affixed itself, an aura cherished and embellished by his great-grandson, who made him the model for Colonel John Sartoris in *Flags in the Dust* and *The Unvanquished*. W. C. Falkner was Faulkner's forebear not only as a hero in the war that forever dramatized the character of the South but also as an author. For Colonel Falkner, amibitious on every side of his active life, wrote a best-seller, *The White Rose of Memphis*. He was at once a frontier brawler, mixed up in several murderous shoot-outs in the last of which he lost his own life, and an entrepreneurial businessman who, after the debacle of the Confederate defeat, tried to revive the Mississippi economy by rebuilding the railroad the Yankees had destroyed. A complex man, fierce, competitive, sentimental, talented, unyielding. But two generations down the line his grandson, William Faulkner's father Murry, was something of a bumbler, a ne'er-do-very-well whose own father set him up in one soon-to-fail enterprise after another. The family was widely ramified with siblings and in-laws, all of whom came well connected in the decades-thin history of antebellum Mississippi.[25]

25. Biographical details of Colonel W. C. Falkner are given fully in Blotner, *Faulkner: A Biography*, I, 14–50.

The intensity, the amplitude of historical detail, the sympathy given by Faulkner to the theme of the ruin of the aristocratic class come with the territory, for much more than any other section the South had actually experienced a class structure in which a landed squirearchy controlled the political, economic, and personal destinies of the region. Although the antebellum planter class in Mississippi was essentially a one- or two-generation aristocracy, in such a society the self-made man—who is in fact the basis for the metamorphic folk hero—is by definition a parvenu. Those who possess wealth, holdings, privilege, position, and power are quick to erect self-protective barriers against the interloper who arrives without the baggage of a history, a family, or a past. When a man like Thomas Sutpen (in *Absalom, Absalom!*) arrives in Yoknapatawpha County with his grandiose plan of setting himself up as the lord of a wilderness fiefdom—a Southern analogue to the original Pyncheon in *The House of the Seven Gables*—such an intruder will never be accepted by those already established on their plantations, with yeomen and slaves in a hierarchy not to be disturbed by a stranger's ambition. Their own ambition, their own fierce pursuits of land, wealth, position, must have been hardly less intense than his, but they got there first and will brook no intrusion by a rootless latecomer.

The Old South placed its slave-owning whites in positions of arbitrary and unchecked power; the order pertained to the poor whites also, who owned no slaves, often no lands either, and were obliged to defer to the values as well as the persons of the master class. This aristocracy had, in the nature of things, certain high and undeviating obligations toward those it owned or led. Faulkner is quite specific in making clear the character of these obligations and the cost, not only to the aristocrats and their descendants but to the South at large, of their flouting or ignoring the responsibilities intrinsic to their position. At the same time he makes it clear that the aristocratic class subscribed to its own code of honor, at once a badge of distinction and a curse, as appears in his chronicle-histories of the Sartorises in *Flags in the Dust* and *The Unvanquished,* the Compsons in *The Sound and the Fury,* and the McCaslins in *Go Down, Moses.*

At the opposite end of the social scale is another of Faulkner's parvenus, another self-made, chameleonic personage. Flem Snopes resembles Sutpen in that he, too, in his different fashion, is enacting the revenge against the stratified society of the South of the descendant of poor white trash. In the course of Faulkner's trilogy (*The Hamlet, The Town, The Mansion*) Flem elevates himself from being the penniless son of a shiftless ex–horse thief and barn burner to being clerk in Varner's store; then he becomes in turn its manager and what the Irish call a gombeen-man, who has all of the dirt farmers in the district in his debt; thence he is cashier in the bank in Jefferson, where he schemes to replace its president, succeeds, and becomes a prominent citizen of the county seat. This progress from rags to riches by an ambitious, bloodless character whose wiles are as intricate as his patience is long, this fulfillment of Poor Richard's wise advice to the journeyman, Faulkner views with loathing. The Horatio Alger attributes of a Flem Snopes lead to success, but not, in Faulkner's world, to heroism. Flem as metamorphic man is Faulkner's version of the twentieth-century commercial man turned devil, a true descendant of Melville's Confidence-Man.

Yoknapatawpha County is also populated by whites who are neither plantation-owning aristocrats nor poor rednecks. These folk, most of whom we meet in *The Hamlet,* include the store owner Will Varner and his son Jody, and sturdy yeomen farmers like Bookwright and Tull. Their presence offers norms of community attitude and behavior against which the pretensions of the ruling class and the outrageousness of Flem and his tribe are measurable.

In addition to the replication of the Fall of Man, another biblical theme appears as a mythical paradigm in Faulkner's work, an executive image of the human condition. This is the *imitatio Christi.* Several of Faulkner's fictional heroes reenact, or try to reenact, the life and sacrifice of Christ, or are seen by their author as conforming, whether knowingly or not, to that archetype. The world being demonstrably fallen, any reprise in contemporary lives of a Gospel paradigm will of necessity be either satirical or parodic; if the parallel is intended seriously despite the evidence of historical fact to the contrary, it will be manipulated as allegory. Yet again, a version of history can include a parallel to the Gospel story, an incomplete and unsuccessful parallel; this approach allows for the representation of historical complexity and gives a tragic dignity to the character's failed attempt to imitate the example of Christ. Faulkner, typically, has written works in all these modes of mythicizing contemporary life, of imbuing biblical paradigms with the texture of historical reality and vice versa. The results are different indeed in three novels that well illustrate the risks and rewards of these strategies. I take them up thematically, in achronological order: the allegory of *A Fable*, the parodic grotesque of *Light in August*, and the replication in *Go Down, Moses* of the attempt of a man to live as it seems to him Christ would have done.

Of course the Gospel paradigm is not treated in isolation in the two last-named novels. Faulkner's sensibility, exploring the richness of his culture, reflects the divisions defined by Matthew Arnold in "Hebraism and Hellenism." Classical antiquity, paganism, and, in the New World, primitivism provide other archetypes and executive metaphors. Here too the tendency is to see the Age of Fable as a Golden Age, and contemporary avatars as also fallen from a now-unattainable grace. These energies of the pagan past do not figure in *A Fable* but are a source of images and metaphors in *Light in August*; in *Go Down, Moses* paganism is a source of pre-Christian spiritual experience.

The last-written of these novels, *A Fable* (1954), is embedded in modern history but not specifically in the history of the South, for, except for the interpolated and extrinsic fable of the race-horse, all the action takes place in France during World War I. That conflict was of course the crucial historical event that defined Faulkner's own generation, as the Civil War had defined that of his great-grandfather half a century earlier. Faulkner himself had volunteered for the R.A.F. but was still taking flight training in Canada when the Armistice was declared. He returned to the University of Mississippi with his flight tunic, swagger stick, and a limp, and encouraged the impression of his having been injured in a crash and of wearing a metal plate in his hip to patch a war wound.[26] The romantic young pilot eager for combat but arriving too late appears in *A Fable,* but otherwise Faulkner's own experience does not directly figure in the work.

The principal character is an unnamed French infantry corporal who, with a dozen accomplices, organizes a rebellion of an entire regiment. After four horrible years of suffering and slaughter, these soldiers disobey an order to attack; their refusal to continue the war spreads among the Allied troops and to the German side. Their general takes this mutiny as a blot on his own honor and presses the Marshal of the Army to order the execution of the entire regiment for dereliction of duty. The Marshal—the fictional equivalent of Marshal Foch—is the corporal's Adversary; in fact he is the corporal's father, having begotten him illegitimately while on duty in the Middle East. On a much grander and more ambitious scale, this novel replays some of the themes and conflicts of Melville's *Billy Budd,* with the military figure of authority (like Captain Vere) representing accommodation to this world, the innocent youth representing a purity of spirit that will not accommodate the world. From this point on the replication in fiction of the Gospels is unequivocal: the corporal's execution between two thieves becomes his Crucifixion, the disappearance of his corpse during a bombardment suggests the empty Tomb, and so on. Faulkner adds an irony by having the corpse chosen by a detail sent to find an unidentified body for interment as the Unknown Soldier.

The pattern, predictable once recognized, is held in abeyance for several hundred pages by a willfully obfuscatory style. Sentences a page long spin almost out of syntactical control, not as expressions of the confusion of one of the characters but as the chosen vehicle of an omniscient narrator who conceals as long as he can—by approaching the theme through the viewpoints of various other characters—that the corporal is the Prince of

26. *Ibid.,* I, 225–26, 229, 231–32, 324.

Peace. Other major characters are similarly nameless—the runner, the sentry—enforcing their identities as archetypal rather than individual persons. But the chief reason why this novel is Faulkner's most ambitious failure was pointed out, soon after the novel appeared, by R. W. B. Lewis: "The trouble with *A Fable* is its lack of complexity in the undefiled purity of the hero, and the undefiled purity with which his person and career repeat those of Jesus. There are symbols in the book, but the corporal, the women, the disciples, the thieves, the judges are not among them. They do not *symbolize* anything; they *are* their originals." This book, Lewis avers, demonstrates "the dramatic unfitness of the unmodulated Christ figure."[27]

Thus despite its realistic evocations of temporal reality, which in themselves are an imaginative feat of considerable magnitude, *A Fable* fails to enclose within its suprahuman structure what Yeats called "The fury and the mire of human veins." Elsewhere, Faulkner has dramatically presented a vision of the Resurrection and an exemplar of muscular Christianity, as in the sermon of the Reverend Shegog in *The Sound and the Fury* and the character of Reverend Goodyhay in *The Mansion.* Shegog and Goodyhay are minor characters whose religion, which we are to take seriously, is counterpointed against the corruption of the world around them; in these works Faulkner does not pretend, as the allegorical structure of *A Fable* requires him and his readers to do, that contemporary reality reveals the replication of the truth of the Gospels.

Over twenty years before *A Fable,* in 1932, Faulkner published a novel that seems designed to demonstrate just the opposite, the total inapplicability of the life of Jesus to contemporary life. For after the Fall comes exile from the Garden and man's durance in our world, the Waste Land. The novelist's invocation of mythic and biblical parallels ironically projects this diminution, the despair, the detritus of our modern condition. Hence the wild discrepancies between mythic and biblical originals and their modern instances in *Light in August* (as, also, in

27. R. W. B. Lewis, *The Picaresque Saint* (Philadelphia, 1959), 218, 210.

Absalom, Absalom!, The Sound and the Fury, Sanctuary, and *Requiem for a Nun*). Readers of *Light in August* have been struck by the correspondence of the initials of its hero with those of Jesus Christ; and surely there is significance in his being given the name Joe Christmas when found abandoned on the orphanage steps on Christmas morning. If this line of inference has any meaning, however, we are asked to accept as a Christ surrogate a bastard and a murderer, who, far from being an ethical example and a leader of men, is an alien against whom everyone's hand is turned and who turns against everyone. His paternity is in doubt to the end—he never knows whether his father was Negro or white—therefore his whole life is a desperate, futile search for wholeness, for self-acceptance. Faulkner has thrust upon this one tortured character the dilemma that Mark Twain dramatized in *Pudd'nhead Wilson* as the fate of two, the black and the white babies switched in the cradle, each growing into a false identity. Joe Christmas acts as a Negro when among whites, as a white man when among Negroes. These considerations have led us far from the Gospels, but there are other tantalizing hints and allusions to the life of Christ, all similarly fraught with contradictions.

It has been suggested that Joe's affair with the prostitute Bobbie alludes to Christ and the fallen woman. Lena Grove seems a Mary figure, a sweet, innocent country girl who carries her illegitimate child while seeking the lover who abandoned her; there is even a conflation of Lena's baby, seen in this connection as a Christ figure, with Joe Christmas, when Joe's grandmother, Mrs. Hines, who is present at Lena's delivery, confuses the new baby with her dead daughter's child Joe. Now, at age thirty-three (or is it thirty-six?), Joe has brutally murdered Joanna Burden, the descendant of an abolitionist and carpetbagger family who had befriended him, taken him as her lover, and, learning that he may be black, turned him into a Negro she can at once patronize and use to fulfill her wild erotic fantasies. By this time Joe has become a bootlegger and has a disciple, Lucas Burch, who betrays him to the sheriff. But the biblical parallels present Lucas, the father of Lena's baby, as a prospective Joseph as well as a Judas. The role of Joseph, however, seems better filled by Byron Bunch, who accepts Lena, loves her, and at the end will doubtless marry her. Thus the novel is riddled with touches suggesting connections between the lives of these poor Mississippi proletarians and the story of Jesus, but we are never clear what those connections can be.

In *Light in August,* Christianity is represented only in grotesque and aberrant forms. There are three ministers in the book, all of them mad. Joe's grandfather, Doc Hines, preaches a God of wrath and hatred. The God of Joe's foster-father McEachern is a God of vengeance. And the God of Byron Bunch's friend, the Reverend Hightower, is a God of self-absorption. Doc Hines, gibbering denunciations of womanfilth, abomination and bitchery, is the evil spirit who blights Joe's life. He murdered Joe's father on mere suspicion that he was black, thrust the baby into an orphanage, became janitor there so he could watch over Joe and pursue him with the doubt of his race; in the end it is Doc Hines preaching hatred to the crowd after Joe is in jail that leads to Joe's murder and mutilation by Percy Grimm. The vengeful Calvinist McEachern, taking the boy out of the orphanage, flogs him for failing to memorize passages from the Bible, and forbids him all normal pleasures. When McEachern pursues and denounces Joe, who has stolen away to meet Bobbie at a dance, the youth brains him with a chair, and begins his endless flight from his own past.

The past is history, and in this book history—the history of the South—is dramatized by the grim determinism with which three chief characters are caught in the toils of their grandfathers' lives. Joe Christmas can never escape from Doc Hines's baleful influence. Hightower is transfixed in time, his imagination unable to move beyond the moment when his grandfather led a doomed Confederate charge, the aging grandson, in his incomprehensible sermons, confusing cavalry with Calvary. Hightower's onanistic daydream represents, historically, the futility of the Confederacy and its irrelevance to the needs of the contemporary South. By the end of the novel Hightower has been rescued from his isolation through the friendship of Byron Bunch and by his helping to deliver Lena's baby. This suggests that he is at last redeemed, or at least that his redemption is possible. The third character obsessed and undone by a grandfather's past is Joanna Burden, who cannot escape her inheritance of his willfulness, his intractability, and his fanatical espousal of the Negro as a cause.

Thus the historicity of *Light in August* dramatizes the determinism that gives the novel its inexorable power. This naturalism, appropriate to a novel about proletarian people written during the Great Depression, would seem incompatible with the tangled hints of allusions to the Christ story. The problems encountered in trying to integrate the latter into the perceived themes of *Light in August* arise, however, from thinking of its mythical or biblical level only in terms of content. In the same year that Berdyaev defined the mythical nature of historical knowledge, T. S. Eliot in his review of *Ulysses* proposed a different yet equally integral role for myth in modern literature.[28] Myth would provide the contemporary writer with the structure of his fiction, as Joyce had taken the form of his novel from the superimposition of contemporaneous reality upon the pattern of *The Odyssey*, each chapter of *Ulysses* being based upon the corresponding book in Homer.

That a similar use of myth informs *Light in August* is the interpretation proposed by Virginia V. Hlavsa. "Faulkner arranged his events and directed the themes in his 21 chapters to parallel the 21 chapters of the St John Gospel. Further, he developed the stories in John by incorporating mythic figures, primitive practice and folk belief from Sir James Frazer's complete *Golden Bough*. In other words, following John sequentially, Faulkner used his chapter themes to reach for the mythic or primitive tradition which he may have thought of as lying behind each story in John, and this with considerable knowledge of Johannine

---

28. T. S. Eliot, "Ulysses, Order, and Myth," *Dial*, LXXV (1923), 480–83.

scholarship." Hlavsa suggests that the novel is structured as is the Gospel of John, the action in its chapters (such as the coming of Lena, and the introduction of a different narrator) paralleling that in corresponding chapters of the Gospel. Further evidence of this correspondence, and of Faulkner's use of Frazer, Hlavsa discovers by searching a concordance of the novel for "key words and groups of high-frequency words," which reveal many verbal parallels, such as those between Hightower and Nicodemus in Chapter 3, and those "linking each vaguely biblical character with an appropriate mythical figure," such as Lena Grove's associations with Mary, the Corn Mother, and Isis.[29] Many of these verbal echoes seem quite tenuous, as though Faulkner were playing a private joke on his readers. Indeed, the dependence of the architecture of the whole work on the Gospel of John, though demonstrable, remains arcane and not, as with *Ulysses,* readily recognized once pointed out.

The source of the novel's strength, as I have indicated, lies not in its parodic distortions of the Gospel or in allusions to the Corn Goddess but in its relentless determinism which so compellingly portrays a modern man torn apart by the region's inheritance of rival fanaticisms of the South and the North. The implied mythical prototype behind Joe Christmas's tragic story is the Waste Land, the ultimate dystopia we have made of our inheritance. The light at the end of the tunnel of Joe's doomed flight is cast by the departure for some other venue of Lena Grove with her newborn son and her faithful friend Byron Bunch, as told to his wife by a travelling furniture dealer who has given them a ride in his wagon. That a novel of such suffering and doom can end in the amused pillow-talk of a happily married couple does provide a ray of hope for mankind. The echoes of Christ's life in Joe's life and death were parodic, satirical, dis-

29. Virginia V. Hlavsa, "St. John and Frazer in *Light in August:* Biblical Form and Mythic Function," *Bulletin of Research in Humanities,* LXXXIII (Spring, 1980), 9–26, quotation from p. 11; Hlavsa, "The Levity of *Light in August,*" in Doreen Fowler and Ann J. Abadie (eds.), *Faulkner and Humor* (Jackson, Miss., 1986), 47–56.

torted, grotesque; perhaps the new baby can lead a life more in *imitatio Christi* than did Joe Christmas. But that would be another story.

Such another story is the one Faulkner wrote and rewrote over the next eight years, culminating in the publication in 1942 of *Go Down, Moses.* Here the character whose life is reminiscent of Christ's mission and sacrifice is no bastard outcast but the heir to a plantation. Isaac McCaslin's given name suggests his role, too, as an averted sacrifice to the Lord. Faulkner in this book abandons irony, such as he had intended in naming Ab Snopes and calling his first chronicle of Snopesism *Father Abraham,* in which Abraham's son is not an Isaac but a Flem.

In what way is Isaac McCaslin an averted sacrifice? The nearest he comes to reenacting the biblical story is in his solitary confrontation with Old Ben, dashing, weaponless, between the great bear's legs to rescue his little fyce, and escaping untouched. The great bear is a complex image, representing the spirit of the wilderness, of olden times, of a primitive nobility beyond that of our world—in short, a numinous, divine essence. His priest, of course, is Sam Fathers, the half-Indian, half-Negro hunter who initiates Isaac into the mysteries of the big woods and the hunt. Sam Fathers is thus Isaac's spiritual father; his own name alludes to his Indian descent as the son of two fathers. Isaac, also, has two fathers—his natural father is Uncle Buck, the comic bachelor of *The Unvanquished* and of "Was" in *Go Down, Moses.* Yet Uncle Buck has left Isaac a spiritual legacy too; for if Isaac learns of primal innocence and the divinity of Nature from Sam Fathers, deciphering the almost illiterate journal of life on the family plantation kept by Uncle Buck and his brother Uncle Buddy he learns also of guilt, his human inheritance. Their journal gradually reveals the original sin lurking behind the prelapsarian boys' life so affectionately and comically dramatized in the opening chapter, "Was." The family history is inexorably tainted by the progenitor Carothers McCaslin's ownership of slaves, his seduction of his slave women, and his committing incest with his half-breed daughter. These sins he had covertly confessed by leaving a bequest in his will to each of his black descendants; still in slavery days, his sons Buck and Buddy had carried repentance a bit further after their father's death by moving into a slave cabin, giving their blacks the run of the big house, and manumitting those who wanted to leave. Isaac, coming of age after Emancipation, takes on the burden of his family's guilt. He tries to expiate these sins by renouncing his inheritance, turning carpenter like Christ, giving up his marriage, and not begetting further descendants to whom the family guilt would be passed.

The imagery surrounding Isaac's double initiation, first into the primal world of the wilderness with its numinous values, then into the tainted world of history with its guilt and responsibilities, is drawn from both biblical and pagan sources. Unlike the satirical and sardonic employment in *Light in August* of references to *The Golden Bough*, paganism in *Go Down, Moses* is treated as a sacral reality with its own rites and practices. Faulkner is not resurrecting classical antiquity but is dramatizing the historical reality of his own county, for one of the blessings he made of his donnée is the nearness to his own day of the time when the land was lived in by Indians with their reverence for the wilderness, their propitiation of the spirits of the game they slew. Sam Fathers is a true high priest, and Isaac proves worthy to become his spiritual heir. To be a spiritual heir of Christ, however, is more difficult still. In the end, Isaac's renunciations seem pointless since he has set no one else an example; his kinsman Roth Edmonds commits yet again the miscegenation and incest (with a distant mulatto cousin) of Carothers McCaslin, thus repeating the original sin of the family. And Isaac has lost something of his own humanity in his pursuit of a superhuman ideal—as the abandoned woman reproves him, holding her baby in her arms, "Old man . . . don't you remember anything you ever knew or felt or even heard about love?"[30]

In *Go Down, Moses*, the theme of Isaac's imitation of Christ is embedded in a historical chronicle of a family over five generations, from the time Mississippi was a wilderness to the

---

30. Faulkner, *Go Down, Moses* (1940; rpr. New York, 1983), 363.

present—1942—when an alienated McCaslin Negro, fled to a Northern city, is executed for murder. The novel thus complexly intertwines several mythic prototypes—the doom of an aristocratic family, exile from Eden, the imitation of Christ—in the historical matrix of the South, with its legacy of the division between the races and its inherited burdens of lust and guilt. History becomes myth, myth becomes history in this work in which, avoiding the parodic bitterness of the earlier *Light in August* and the allegorical simplifications of the later *A Fable*, Faulkner, at the height of his creative powers, successfully fused the representation of reality with his imagination of the experience of the South.

II

THE UNVANQUISHED

Q. *Sir, what book would you advise to read first of yours?*
A. *I would say maybe* The Unvanquished. . . . *Because it's
    easy to read. Compared to the others, I mean.*
                              —Faulkner in the University

THE STORY

The Unvanquished is among Faulkner's most accessible books,
since its straightforward narration has neither the warpings of
time nor the complications of style characteristic of his denser
fictions. Accordingly, among some of its author's most devoted
critics, this book has not enjoyed much respect. Although "the
book does touch, however lightly, on some of the major themes,"
Michael Millgate remarked in his first study of Faulkner, it "gives
little inkling of his greatness"; its excitement "is merely super-
ficial, subsisting . . . almost entirely in the narrative pace, and
the book does not emerge well from a second reading." Giving
The Unvanquished a second reading a few years later, Millgate
concludes that it "remains distinctly a minor work"; "the dis-
criminating reader . . . is likely to find . . . little incentive to read
further in Faulkner's work and few indications of those qualities
which make him a major writer." Not only does the straight-
forwardness of *The Unvanquished* fail to require of the reader a
complex response, as do Faulkner's greater works, but, many
readers agree, it "presents a romanticized and almost entirely
uncritical picture of Southern aristocracy."[1]

1. Michael Millgate, *Faulkner* (New York, 1971), 67, and *The Achievement
of William Faulkner* (1966; rpr. Lincoln, Nebr., 1978), 170; Dorothy Tuck,
Apollo Handbook of Faulkner (New York, 1964), 69.

Other critics have taken *The Unvanquished* seriously enough
to write about it at some length, although they frequently skirt
the question of whether the work is a successful novel, or an im-
portant one, or indeed any good at all. A chapter in John Pilkington's *The Heart of Yoknapatawpha* gives a clear and sensible account of the genesis of the book, its transformation from short
stories that Faulkner referred to as "trash" into a novel rewritten
with considerable care, and Pilkington offers a fair statement of
the significance of the work in the context of Faulkner's sense of
the history of the South. Others have explored or defended *The
Unvanquished* with more particular ends in view. Waggoner's
early favorable reading defines the moral code the book exemplifies; Walker finds the novel a thicket of symbols whose
significance reinforces the tradition of the Old South; Miller
discusses it as Faulkner's only treatment of the Civil War; Mem-
mott and Messenger explore the theme of action as play in the
work; and Taylor finds *The Unvanquished* to be a foreshadow-
ing of the racial theme in *Absalom, Absalom!*, which Faulkner
was writing at the same time.[2]

My concern with *The Unvanquished* is, first, to save the tale
from the teller. However derogatorily Faulkner referred to his
short stories, written for money, the book that resulted from his
revisions and additions to those tales is not "trash." And it is
certainly not a simple defense of the Southern aristocracy or a
sentimental treatment of antebellum times.[3] Random House
published *The Unvanquished* in the hope that Faulkner's treat-

2. John Pilkington, *The Heart of Yoknapatawpha* (Jackson, Miss., 1981),
189–216; Hyatt H. Waggoner, *William Faulkner: From Jefferson to the World*
(Lexington, Ky., 1959), 170–83; William E. Walker, "*The Unvanquished*—The
Restoration of Tradition," in W. F. Walker and R. L. Welker (eds.), *Reality in
Myth* (Nashville, 1964), 275–97; Douglas T. Miller, "Faulkner and the Civil
War: Myth and Reality," *American Quarterly*, XV (1962), 200–209; A. James
Memmot, "Sartor *Ludens:* The Play Element in *The Unvanquished*," *Missis-
sippi Quarterly*, XXIX (1976), 375–87; Christian K. Messenger, *Sport and the
Spirit of Play in American Fiction* (New York, 1981), 262–74; Walter Taylor,
Faulkner's Search for a South (Urbana, 1983), 40.

3. See Joseph Blotner, *Faulkner: A Biography* (2 vols.; New York, 1974), II, 951.

ment of the South during the Civil War would rival in popularity his fellow townsman Stark Young's *How Red the Rose* and Margaret Mitchell's *Gone with the Wind*, both recently published and made into popular motion pictures.[4] In fact *The Unvanquished* is simpler on its surfaces than in its themes; even in writing what started out as a string of potboilers, Faulkner, whose imagination at any given moment contained the whole of the Yoknapatawpha saga in potentiality, created a work of moral and thematic complexity.

Faulkner imposed a unifying structure upon his series of discrete anecdotes. This structure links them in a series of repeated actions and resonant images that together help embody the meaning of the book. *The Unvanquished* tells several interconnected stories, the most significant of which embodies the initiation of Bayard Sartoris into the responsibilities and meaning of his life. The action begins when he is twelve and follows him intermittently until he is twenty-four. The time extends from 1861 to 1873; the venue is chiefly the Sartoris plantation in northern Mississippi during and after the Civil War. At first the war is distant—the boy's father, Colonel John Sartoris, is away with his troops. His mother is dead, and his grandmother, Rosa Millard, is in charge of the place. Invasion is imminent; the colonel returns momentarily but makes a hair's breadth escape from his pursuers.

A complicated plot involves Granny Millard's means of helping the family and her neighbors survive during this dire time. Outraged by the pillage of the family silver (a Sartoris slave had betrayed its hiding place and gone off with the conquerors) and by the confiscation of their mules, Granny, with Bayard and his Negro chum Ringo, journeys right into the Union camp to demand return of her goods, beasts, and slaves. The Northern commander grants her request, but an adjutant, mishearing the names of the mules, Old Hundred and Tinney, writes a requisition for 110 mules, 110 slaves, and 10 chests. Despite her pro-

4. Pilkington, *The Heart of Yoknapatawpha*, 292.

testations Granny is ushered from the camp with these many accoutrements.[5]

Back home, in collaboration with Ab Snopes, a shiftless horse trader who has evaded military service, Rosa Millard supports her whole neighborhood by using forged copies of the original requisition to retrieve mules from Union regiments, which Snopes then sells to other Northern outfits at a distance from where the mules were obtained. In this manner, enacting the widespread folklore theme of selling gullible victims the same goods over and over again, Granny Millard, as representative of Southern women on the home front in the occupied South, outwits the enemy army.[6] After many such expeditions, Snopes persuades Granny to try to commandeer the stolen horses of a night-riding bushwhacker named Grumby. In the course of her

5. Rosa Millard's successful venture into enemy headquarters seems highly improbable. Is it likely that a wagonload of Rebel civilians on such an errand would actually be permitted to address the company commander? Curiously, Granny Millard's adventure is paralleled in a memoir, "A Beauty Spot on the Northern Side" (Typescript in WPA Federal Writers Project files, Mississippi State Department of Archives and History, Jackson). This memoir, "told to the writer (Willa Johnson) by Narcissa Keene Johnson," is rewritten, absent its genteel stylistic flourishes, by Hubert Creekmore, also on the Writers Project, in a synoptic piece, "Tales of the War," intended for publication (but not used) in the *Mississippi Guide.* Mrs. Johnson tells how, as the sixteen-year-old bride of a Confederate colonel, she brought her baby and her English governess through the Union lines at Vicksburg to request permission to cross the river to join her husband, who had never seen his child. Rudely refused by orderlies, she was given a hand-written permit by General MacPherson himself. Since Mrs. Johnson's account is stamped "Received October 7, 1938," while Faulkner's "Raid" appeared in *The Saturday Evening Post* on 3 November 1934, one cannot categorically say that hers is an independent family legend. At any rate, at ninety she was willing to attribute to the Union commander gentlemanly courtesy such as Faulkner reports of Colonel Dick.

6. See, *e.g.,* "The Turner Coonskin," in Vance Randolph, *Sticks in the Knapsack and Other Ozark Folk Tales* (New York, 1958), 115–16, 162–63, where other versions of this motif are cited (Motif K258.4, "Merchant buys the same article several times from the same or different sellers," in Ernest W. Baughman, *A Comparative Study of Folktales in England and North America* [Ann Arbor, 1954]). Randolph's and Baughman's citations show the tale known in Arkansas, Missouri, Illinois, and Florida.

dealings with Ab Snopes she has been to some extent corrupted by him; now, stooping from her height of rectitude (in which she is shown as self-willed and arrogant, as well as benevolent), she allows Snopes to persuade her. When she rashly presents herself, Grumby kills her. Bayard and Ringo, accompanied by an elderly neighbor, Uncle Buck McCaslin, set out to avenge her murder. After an arduous two-month chase in which Uncle Buck is wounded and must leave the boys to carry on, they track Grumby down. Ringo attacks him with a jackknife as Bayard kills him with Uncle Buck's pistol.

Intrinsic to the theme of Bayard Sartoris' initiation into life is his—and our—measuring of the ethos of his class, the aristocracy. We see exhibited in various degrees in the actions of Colonel Sartoris, Rosa Millard, Drusilla Hawk, and Uncle Buck McCaslin the two faces of their ethos: responsibility and honor. *Noblesse oblige* is expected of the aristocrat, a courtesy toward those whom Providence has decreed he should lead. Mingled with other personal traits in Colonel Sartoris, we see his concern to bring his region and its people back to prosperity through the rebuilding of the railroad after the war.

Coincident with all of this is the development of another theme that dramatizes the effects of the war upon the civilians of the South. Women are thrust into men's roles as heads of households and communities, as we see Granny Millard disciplining the two boys and the Negroes, running her complicated mule-stealing scam, and distributing her share of its proceeds to the poor black and white dirt farmers scratching a living from the devastated land. When the Sartoris place has been destroyed, Granny, Bayard and Ringo pay a visit to their kinsfolk the Hawks, who, like them, after the burning of their mansion, are living in half of a Negro cabin, the white and the black folk divided by a sheet hung as a curtain. There Granny and the boys find Cousin Drusilla, whose fiancé was killed at Shiloh, and who in a different fashion from Rosa Millard will be desexed by the war. She puts on a man's uniform and runs off to serve as a soldier in John Sartoris' regiment. After the war Drusilla returns with the colonel and helps him rebuild the plantation. Her mother, outraged by Drusilla's flaunting of the conventions and decencies in not only wearing men's clothing but living in unmarried state with her cousin, enlists the ladies of the Sartoris' neighborhood to compel Drusilla to marry John Sartoris. As they go to town for their wedding—it is election day—the colonel finds that two northern carpetbaggers, the Burdens, have arranged to have an illiterate freed slave elected town marshall. Responding to the community's outrage, the colonel confronts the Burdens, who draw their guns and fire, missing him; he shoots them both. After further complications the wedding of this reluctant couple is held at last. Drusilla has been desexed by her grief, hardship, and suffering. When Sartoris is killed by his partner Redmond, Drusilla is consumed by bloodlust, exhorting Bayard to murder his father's killer.

Yet another theme interconnected with the foregoing concerns the relationship of the races before, during, and after Emancipation. The Sartoris Negroes are well treated and, except for Loosh, are loyal to the family. Loosh, who has heard through the slaves' underground intelligence network of the Confederate defeat at Vicksburg, is resentful of his bondage. When the Yankees come it is he who leads them to the Sartoris silver and, with his unwilling wife Philadelphy, follows the conquerors. All over Mississippi other Negroes, naïvely confusing the promises of freedom with the promise of their religion, form lemminglike columns of chanting, wailing pilgrims seeking to cross the river Jordan. The Union troops are dismayed by this; Southerners, like Granny and Drusilla, are compassionate to them, but no one can help them in their delusion. The postwar episodes of the attempted fraudulent election and the depredations against innocent freed Negroes by Grumby's band of desperadoes suggest the effects on the South, both in country and in town, of the breakdown of custom and civil authority.

Posed against these images of social dissolution is the friendship between Bayard and Ringo—who is so much a member of the family that he too calls Rosa Millard "Granny." Theirs has been described as a Tom and Huck relationship, but since neither for long has Tom Sawyer's romantic illusions or pretensions they might better be thought of as Huck and Huck: two resourceful boys in a hard situation. But their idyllic relationship cannot survive boyhood: when they are grown, Bayard becomes a man, a moral sophisticate; Ringo is no longer his equal but his servant, and has not had the same opportunities for the development of his spirit.

THE WAR

Bayard's initiation is structured around three episodes in which he expects, or is expected, to kill another man: a killing attempted, a killing achieved, and a killing averted. The first (in "Ambuscade") is Bayard and Ringo's attempt to shoot the first Yankee they see. Home on the farm, to them battles had a storybook, gamelike quality; as the tale opens, we see the two boys playing at war with a map scratched in the earth to represent the siege of Vicksburg, which they do not yet know (although Loosh knows) has fallen to the enemy. When they see a lone Yankee soldier riding toward them around the curve in the road, they rush into the house for the musket, and, in a trance of suspended animation, Bayard pulls the trigger with his eyes closed. Then Ringo sees coming around the bend "the whole army" of which the lone rider had been harbinger. In a panic the boys rush inside as Yankee troops pursue them. Granny motions them under her spread skirts as she sits in a rocking chair denying, first to a sergeant, then to his colonel, that there are any boys on the place. The only damage done is the Union soldiers' killing of the presumed victim's wounded horse—on which they had placed wagers for the next race. So the attempted killing was no killing, and even the horse figured not as a beast of war but in a diversion, a game. The Yankee colonel, himself the father of three boys, sees through Granny Millard's subterfuge but with ironical courtesy lets her protect the boys; even a Yankee can be a gentleman. The tale ends on a trivializing note: because the boys had told Granny "We shot the bastud," she punishes them for their "obscene language" by making them wash their mouths with soap and water.

Nothing could be less like this farcical playing at war than Bayard's second experience of pulling a trigger on another man. As we learn in "Riposte in Tertio," by the war's end, with the Union Army departing, Granny Millard had given away nearly all her share—or what Ab Snopes had led her to believe was her fair share—of the proceeds of the great sell-back of requisitioned mules. The game was dangerous, for there was always the risk that the Yankee regiments would be on the lookout for an old woman with two boys and a forged requisition. Ultimately, Ab Snopes tempts Granny into one more caper, persuading her that she should keep the proceeds this time for her own kin. He knows where Grumby has lodged four stolen horses that she can requisition using the name of Confederate General Forrest, with whom Grumby claims to have served. Bayard tries to dissuade her from this perilous enterprise, but he is only fifteen, and she is secure in her assumption that "these were Southern men and, therefore, there would not even be any risk . . . because Southern men would not harm a woman, even if the letter failed to work."[7] So Bayard and Ringo ride in a wagon with her the sixty miles to an old cotton compress, knowing "that Grumby, or whoever he was, was a coward and . . . nobody dared frighten a coward" (172–73). Granny walks down the dark lane alone— and when she fails to return Bayard and Ringo rush after her, arriving too late: the shack is vacant save where Granny lies collapsed on the floor, the air heavy with the smell of powder.

In "Vendée," Bayard, accompanied by Ringo and Uncle Buck McCaslin, sets out to avenge Granny's death. In a creek bottom near Snopes's cabin they find a pen just like the one Ab had helped build on the Sartoris place, holding the four horses he had described as belonging to Grumby. So Ab Snopes had sent Granny to her death, to get her out of his way while he continued the

---

7. Faulkner, *The Unvanquished* (1938; rpr. New York, 1966), 171. Pagination of further citations will be indicated parenthetically in the text.

mule- and horse-stealing business. Bayard now thinks Ab *is* Grumby, but Uncle Buck knows better: "He's the one that's going to show us where Grumby is" (184). The three set out "along the known roads and the unknown (and sometimes unmarked) trails and paths, in the wet and the iron frost" (186) on a chase that lasts from December through February. This arduous manhunt reflects Faulkner's own fascination with and skill at stalking games, in which, in his twenties, he had led boys in Oxford.[8]

As they close in on Snopes and Grumby's gang, a bearded stranger rides up to their campfire. When Ringo lets slip that they are seeking two men, he warns them to stick to Snopes—he himself is after Grumby. Remounting his horse, the stranger pulls his pistol and shoots Uncle Buck in the arm. The next day they come upon Snopes, tied up by the Grumby gang and left where the three would find him. Bayard beats Snopes, and Buck gives him a ritual whipping, but they do not kill the craven. Now Buck, whose arm has begun to fester, must abandon the hunt for Grumby; giving Bayard his pistol, he returns home with Snopes. The boys press on past a grisly warning—a hanged Negro with a note attached to his corpse: Grumby's *"last woning . . . Turn back. The barer of this my promise and garntee."* Beneath that, in a finer hand, is an unsigned postscript by their recent visitor, who writes he has no *"scruples re children"* but will give them *"one more chance. Take it, and some day become a man. Refuse it, and cease even to be a child"* (203). Undeterred, the next day they ride on until Ringo's mule shies and a man steps out of the bushes: the stranger who had shot Uncle Buck. Two more men emerge, one with his arms bound behind him. "You want Grumby. Here he is." The bearded stranger, whose companion has everyone covered, reveals that he is the leader of the outlaws, and that Grumby had scrubbed the "good thing" they had going by murdering an old woman and setting the whole country in arms against them. He throws a pistol to the ground,

---

8. Calvin S. Brown, Jr., "Billy Faulkner, My Boyhood Friend," in James W. Webb and A. Wigfall Green (eds.), *William Faulkner of Oxford* (Baton Rouge, 1965), 44–45.

orders his man to cut Grumby free, then they wheel and ride into the woods. Grumby lunges for the pistol and fires three shots after them before turning to face Bayard and Ringo. He pretends he's out of bullets—"Durn my hide for letting Matt Bowden fool me into emptying my pistol at him"—but Bayard knows Grumby has two more shots. In their tense confrontation "there was a bird somewhere—a yellowhammer—I had been hearing it all the time," until suddenly Bayard sees two orange flashes and the gray coat "swelling slow down on me" (208–209), as Grumby rushes him. Struggling beneath Grumby, he sees Ringo leap on the outlaw's back with his open pocketknife. As Bayard frees his pistol Grumby tries to run, but the boy holds it steady and fires.

The boys return home quickly, for "what we had to carry now, wrapped in a piece of the skirt of Grumby's coat, didn't weigh anything" (210). In the rain—it has rained all throughout this tale—they ride past the ruined town and tie up their mules by Granny's grave. Someone has put up a headboard.

The earth had sunk too now, after two months; it was almost level now, like at first Granny had not wanted to be dead either but now she had begun to be reconciled. We unwrapped it, from the jagged square of stained faded gray cloth and fastened it to the board. "Now she can lay good and quiet," Ringo said.

"Yes," I said. And then we both began to cry.   (211)

Bayard's style throughout has been laconic—this is the first sign or admission of emotion. Arriving home, the boys are told by Louvinia, the cook: "Hit done finished! All but the surrendering. And now Marse John done home" (212). Drusilla has come too, and both are out searching for the boys with Uncle Buck leading them. Bayard and Ringo awaken with the colonel and Drusilla clasping them, while Uncle Buck hollers:

Not only tracked down and caught him but brought back the actual proof of it to where Rosa Millard could rest quiet . . . The proof and the expiation! . . . When me and John Sartoris and Drusilla rode up to that old compress, the first thing we see was that murdering scoundrel pegged out on the door to it like a coon hide, all except the right hand.

"And if anybody wants to see that, too," I told John Sartoris, "just let them ride into Jefferson and look on Rosa Millard's grave!" Ain't I told you he is John Sartoris' boy? Hey? Ain't I told you?   (213)

Many a reader has been repelled by the gruesome conclusion to "Vendée." Millgate finds in this "violent and somewhat repulsive" story Bayard and Ringo's "vindictiveness and savagery almost equal to" Grumby's; Taylor calls Grumby's mutilation a "grisly triumph"; and Pilkington maintains that "'Vendée' strains the credulity of the reader. . . . The earlier stories contain no hint or suggestion that these two fifteen-year-old boys . . . could or would track and kill a man of Grumby's ruthlessness, nail his body to a compress door, cut off his hand, and fasten it to a board above her grave." These responses all seem predicated on accepting Grumby's mutilation as Bayard's idea. Thus, "in 'Vendée' Bayard emerges as an avenger out of the Old Testament. Overnight, he has not only accepted the frontier notion of personal justice but also carried it to the extreme of mutilation. . . . That Bayard, as an older man remembering this event in his life, makes no explanation or comment upon it contributes to the basic weakness of the story."[9]

It is indeed a shock to find the lad whose mouth was washed with soap whenever he said a naughty word become "an avenger out of the Old Testament"—though indeed Bayard (and Ringo) has exacted more than an eye for an eye, the severed hand serving, as Uncle Buck had hollered, as "the proof and the expiation!" It is not precisely accurate, however, to aver that Bayard has suddenly "accepted the frontier notion of personal justice," for it has been manifested all around him, in his father's attitudes and behavior and, at this point, in Uncle Buck's. And how did Uncle Buck McCaslin, who was not present at the killing, know where Colonel Sartoris and Drusilla might look to find Grumby's missing hand? It is indeed unlikely that Bayard and Ringo thought of this expiation, this proof, by themselves—for Cleanth Brooks is right in calling these "acts too savage to be

9. Millgate, *Faulkner*, 68; Taylor, *Faulkner's Search for a South*, 96; Pilkington, *The Heart of Yoknapatawpha*, 206.

those of a fifteen-year-old boy . . . gently nurtured."[10] We know, however, that Bayard's first impulse was to borrow a pistol and avenge Granny's murder, though he didn't yet know who killed her or how to find him. Uncle Buck thrust himself into the boys' expedition. When he chortles at the end, "Ain't I told you he is John Sartoris' boy?" it is usually thought not only that Bayard has shown courage like his father's but that this indicates how Colonel Sartoris would have acted in similar circumstances; Bayard's bloody revenge on Grumby is identified with his father's adherence to frontier justice, the code duello. There is no doubt that the colonel, who later in this book kills several men on much less provocation, would surely have slain Grumby on sight, but "pegged [him] out on the door . . . like a coon hide, all except the right hand"? That does not seem John Sartoris' style. Whose style is it, then?

At no point in "Vendée" are we told all that Uncle Buck McCaslin said to his two young companions during the forty days and nights they spent together in the wilderness. The conversation reported had to do with his locating Ab Snopes, his dealing with the arrival of Matt Bowden, and so on. But surely there was much said that Bayard does not remember, or chooses not to tell, or has suppressed. When we consider Buck's character, as given, there is much reason for us to fill in a blank or two and assume that it was he who expostulated at a campfire deep in the woods, or muttered as he rode his mule through the rainy river bottom, what *he* would do—what Bayard *ought* to do—to Grumby when they caught him.

Uncle Buck is presented as a man at once hot-blooded and observant of codes and rules, whether socially sanctioned or made up by himself (and his brother Uncle Buddy). When John Sartoris was elected colonel of the regiment, only one of the McCaslin twins could go, "and they decided themselves which one it would be . . . in the one possible manner in which the victor could know he had earned his right, the loser that he had been conquered by a better man" (56): they dealt a hand of poker, fac-

10. Cleanth Brooks, *William Faulkner: The Yoknapatawpha Country* (New Haven, 1963), 86.

ing each other with a look Bayard remembers as that of some long-dead Puritan preacher. Uncle Buddy won and is serving in Virginia when Buck first sees the boys and Granny Millard in their wagon on the road. His comic banter telling a Confederate captain of the exploits of Colonel Sartoris concludes with his advising Bayard to say to his father: "I said to . . . kill the blue-bellied sons of bitches. Kill them!" (61). Uncle Buck takes upon himself the responsibility of seeing that Granny's murder is properly avenged, saving the boys from their initial error—wanting to kill Snopes instead of Grumby— and then skillfully leading them to Grumby's lair. The violence of the symbolic revenge the boys exact upon the already-dead Grumby bespeaks the vehemence of Buck McCaslin's feelings as well as their own bottomless grief and rage. It is hard indeed for mere boys to have to take upon themselves so horrible a burden, but who else is there to bring Grumby to justice? The South is in tatters, its society shattered, its communal institutions destroyed, and ruthless marauders like Matt Bowden's minions terrorize the poverty-stricken farmers, widows, and freedmen. The land is lawless, and if there is to be any justice at all, it must be the frontier variety of personal vengeance for wrongs suffered.

But there is still that business of the severed hand. How else can the spirit of the murdered woman be quelled but by leaving tied to the headboard of her grave "the proof and the expiation," the hand that pulled the trigger? This has the look, the feel, of an old superstition, one related to Baughman's folktale motif "Return from the dead to avenge a murder" or "Murdered person cannot rest in grave," but I have not found any exact parallel.[11] If there is one, it is probably of Scottish and Appalachian provenience.

Calling the chapter in which these events occur "Vendée" is Faulkner's way of universalizing the sufferings, terror, and revenge he plots in Mississippi. The allusion is to the Wars of the Vendée, a campaign in the south of France of resistance to the Revolution in 1793. In a backward, agrarian region the peasants

11. Baughman, *A Comparative Study of Folktales of England and North America*, Motifs E234.3, E413.

refused to be drafted into the republican army and formed a militia of their own. After initial successes—they overran Samur, Cholet, and several other towns—they were themselves decisively defeated at Savenay by the end of the year. The struggle was marked by massacres, bloody battles, torture of prisoners, the breakdown of order in a rural region. Faulkner most likely learned of the Vendée from Balzac's novel *Les Chouans*. Faulkner owned a 30-volume set of Balzac's novels; the only one of which he had a second copy (in a different translation) is *Les Chouans*; the title refers to Breton smugglers who sided with the Vendéans.[12] Although the Vendéans were suppressed they remained unreconstructed, rising again during the Hundred Days, when their revolt weakened Napoleon's forces and so contributed to his defeat at Waterloo; and yet again, in 1832, they rallied for an abortive royalist rebellion. In the Wars of the Vendée Faulkner found, seventy years before Vicksburg, a close anticipation of the spirit and the plight of the Confederacy, an earlier war in which the regional loyalties of a southern country people and their impassioned desire not to change their traditional way of life led to great sufferings and heroism in a futile cause.

PEACE

The third stage in Bayard's initiation into manhood seems a repetition of the second. This time it is his father who has been murdered, shot to death by a former business partner, and the pressure to avenge this crime which, in the earlier instance of Granny Millard's death Bayard felt within himself as though an instinct in his blood, is now exerted upon him by just about everyone he knows: it is expected of him by George Wyatt and the other veterans of the colonel's regiment, by Ringo, even by the judge in whose home Bayard boards while studying law at the university. Most of all, he is urged to take revenge by

12. Joseph Blotner (comp.), *William Faulkner's Library* (Charlottesville, 1964), 90–92. Both copies of *Les Chouans* are autographed by Faulkner (not all his books were signed), suggesting that he did not want them to go astray.

Drusilla, his young stepmother. In "An Odor of Verbena," however, there are two circumstances differing from those of "Vendée": first, the war is over and the South is trying to reconstitute
itself as a civilized society; and second, where Bayard was fifteen
when Grumby shot Rosa Millard, he is now twenty-four. He has
lived through a great deal, has observed his father, whom he
honors, respects, and loves, in both war and peace, and has had
time to reflect upon his own experiences and his father's, and the
consequences of what they have done.

Buck McCaslin's bloody-mindedness is given us as typical of
the Southern cavalrymen whom Colonel Sartoris had led. General Sherman described the type: "War suits them, and the ras-
cals are brave, fine riders, bold to rashness, and dangerous sub-
jects in every sense . . . they are the most dangerous set of men
that the war has turned loose upon the world." Colonel Sartoris
himself is sui generis, a larger-than-life evocation of the reckless
bravery and touchy sense of honor characteristic of the Southerners of his class. The colonel is modelled upon the life and
family legends of Colonel W. C. Falkner, a veteran of the Mexican War who, like Colonel Sartoris, in the Civil War was elected
colonel of a militia he organized, then, after being voted out of
his colonelcy a year later, returned home and organized a second
company of partisan rangers. In his first engagement Falkner
fought with such tenacity that a correspondent quoted General
Beauregard as shouting, "Go ahead, you hero with the black
plume; *history shall never forget you!*" [13] But this was the apogee
of Falkner's military career; his subsequent actions were less
stellar, and his military exploits dwindled to obscurity.[14] Rein-
carnated in his great-grandson's imagination as Colonel John
Sartoris, however, he is undefeatable. How could he be otherwise,
since his feats are hoary with the triumphs of many tellings. Racing ahead of Bayard and Ringo on his great horse Jupiter, he suddenly sees, as he reaches a hilltop, a Yankee regiment encamped

13. General Sherman to General Halleck, 1863; Brooks, *William Faulkner:
The Yoknapatawpha Country,* 76, cites the passage from Edmund Wilson's *Patriotic Gore.*

14. See Blotner, *Faulkner: A Biography,* I, 20–32.

below. "Surround them, boys! Don't let a man escape!" (75) he shouts to his force of two, and when the enemy troops surrender he makes them strip down to their underclothes, then lets them slip away in the night, leaving their horses behind. When the tables are turned on the colonel—he has come home and the Yankees surround his house—he escapes by a ruse equally traditional; pretending to be a deaf simpleton on his front porch, he says he'll take them to Colonel Sartoris but has to go inside to get his boots, then slips out the back way to the barn and mounts Jupiter barebacked, bursting out of the barn and escaping.[15]

The imagery surrounding Colonel Sartoris in these exploits is heroic, even mythic. Early on in "Ambuscade" his son sees him "standing in the stirrups above the smoke-colored diminishing thunderbolt" as he rides away to rejoin his troops (14). One critic suggests that "it is in just these moments that Colonel John appears most god-like—in the moments when he is equated with Jupiter, the horse, in the role of master or manipulator of the mana so necessary to the successful completion of the ritual struggle."[16] Seen through the boy's eyes, his father is larger than life; he appears so to Uncle Buck McCaslin, whose ranting description of the colonel is in the exaggerative mode of folk humor ("John Sartoris is a damned confounded selfish coward, askeered to stay at home where the Yankees might get him . . . he has to raise him up another batch of men to protect him every time he gets within a hundred foot of a Yankee brigade. Scouring all up and down the country, finding Yankees to dodge," 59–60). Colonel Sartoris thinks of himself in heroic terms, too, for he had doubtless read the sets in his own bookcase—a complete Sir Walter Scott, Fenimore Cooper, and Dumas, as well as Napoleon's maxims. (Also, Coke, the Koran, Josephus, Jeremy Taylor, and a history of werewolves in the British Isles; a library the equal of that of the Grangerfords in *Huckleberry Finn*.) It is with some

15. Ante Aarne and Stith Thompson (eds.), *Motif Index of Folk Literature* (6 vols.; Bloomington, 1958), Motif K700, "Capture by deception"; K1810, "Deception by disguise"; K523.1, "Escape by shamming madness."

16. Walter Brylowski, *Faulkner's Olympian Laugh: Myth in the Novels* (Detroit, 1968), 122.

surprise that Bayard notices his father's actual stature to be not especially prepossessing—the man's bearing, like his actions, enlarges his effect on the beholder. For all his heroics, what Colonel Sartoris is seen and reported doing involves largely the stealing of Yankee horses, the very line of warfare which his mother-in-law Rosa Millard will, with the help of Bayard, Ringo, and Ab Snopes, make her own.

More closely resembling his real-life antecedent is Colonel Sartoris' quickness to avenge an insult. By the time W. C. Falkner was thirty he had stabbed a fellow soldier who drew a revolver on him, had shot the first victim's friend, with whom he had had an argument, and had accepted a challenge to a duel from the brother of his first antagonist. It is typical of the spirit of the times and place that when brought to trial for the two murders, Falkner was acquitted of both.[17]

Christopher Newman, the veteran Civil War officer in Henry James's *The American*, had, in 1877, mourned the wasteful death of his friend Henri de Cintré, killed by a German in a senseless duel over a point of honor which Newman could not but find insignificant. Both the Frenchman's sense of personal honor and his settling of an insult by a duel appear foreign, barbarous customs of king-ridden Europe to this veteran of the northern side. Along the Mississippi Valley, however, this sense of honor and this means of defending it were commonplace. In *Life on the Mississippi* (1883) Mark Twain attributes the survival there of the code duello to the sham medievalism of the South, the Sir Walter Scott influence "curiously confused and commingled" with "the wholesome civilization of the nineteenth century." In his fortieth chapter he gives a fatuously genteel description of a ladies' college: "Believing the Southern to be the highest type of civilization this continent has seen, the young ladies are trained according to the Southern ideas of delicacy, refinement, womanhood, religion and propriety." This is savagely undercut by a long footnote citing newspaper descriptions of cold-blooded murders and feuds in which the trigger-

17. Blotner, *Faulkner: A Biography*, I, 16–19.

happy aggressors—among them a former general—are of course acquitted. A dozen years later, in *Pudd'nhead Wilson*, Mark Twain is still caricaturing the Southern gentry and its chivalric pretensions: in Chapter XII, "The Shame of Judge Driscoll," scapegrace Tom humiliates his putative uncle by taking Count Luigi Capello to court for kicking him, instead of issuing a challenge to a duel. In Chapter XIV, Roxy, Tom's Negro mother, is as outraged as was Judge Driscoll on learning that her flesh and blood has disgraced himself by turning to the law instead of having the courage his honor demands. The Driscoll honor is assuaged in the end, for the judge issues the challenge. The duel of course is a farce in which all the bystanders are wounded but the duellists themselves are unscathed.

Before examining Colonel Sartoris' imbroglios, it is well to clarify the intermingled confusion of duelling and murdering a man in the street. The former is a ritual, socially sanctioned, by which an insult is avenged or nullified by consent of the injuring party to the challenge of the injured. Weapons, place, and time of confrontation are chosen by agreement; negotiations are conducted by friends of the principals who attend the duel as seconds; often a physician accompanies them. This rigmarole is at once barbarous and civil in that a private vengeance is sought outside the law, but it is done in accordance with a gentlemen's code. To conduct such a duel requires a social framework to support its rules and roles. Such was sometimes the case on the American frontier, whether sheriffs and lawyers were at hand or not; but more often, the duel and its code degenerated into pulling a gun at the drop of an insult. The gentleman's touchy personal honor survived, but the civility of negotiations by seconds—in the course of which many a duel, like Colonel Falkner's, was averted—disappeared, and the response to an insult, whether genuine or only presumptive, was instant gunplay.

The tendency among those who responded in this way was to take the law into their own hands all the time. If Judge Driscoll in *Pudd'nhead Wilson* holds recourse to the law to be beneath the dignity of an FFV, Colonel Falkner seems not to have even considered such a course. After the war Bayard notices "Father's

violent and ruthless dictatorialness and will to dominate" that
lead to his falling out with Redmond, his partner in the rebuilding of the railroad, whom he baits and taunts unfairly (258).
With lesser persons John Sartoris is more peremptory still;
carrying bags of gold to pay his railroad workers, one Saturday
Sartoris kills "a hill man who had been in the first infantry regiment when it voted Father out of command: and we never get to
know if the man actually intended to rob Father or not because
Father had shot too quick" (154–55). This is an egregious murder; the victim's widow contemptuously flings in the colonel's
face the money he has sent her, perhaps as a guilt payment.

John Sartoris is involved in another fatal gunplay when he
confronts two carpetbaggers to prevent the election they have
arranged of an illiterate freedman as town marshall. They draw
and fire, missing him, but his shots are on the mark.[18] After this,
Sartoris does turn to judicial process, insisting on turning himself in and making bond. "Don't you see we are working for
peace through law and order?" (239) he says to George Wyatt, a
veteran of his regiment.[19] Wyatt later tells Bayard, explaining
why Sartoris taunts Redmond for not having served in the army

18. As Pilkington remarks, Faulkner told this tale thrice over, varying the
circumstances between this version and the earlier ones in *Sartoris* (and *Flags in
the Dust*) and *Light in August*, where the carpetbaggers appear as Joanna Burden's grandfather and half-brother. "What is remarkable about the three versions
is that Faulkner has presented three different approaches—even three different
sets of 'facts'—to the same event, but left the 'truth' for the reader to establish
for himself" (*The Heart of Yoknapatawpha*, 208).

19. In "Tales of War," Hubert Creekmore tells a parallel story concerning
General Nathan Bedford Forrest. After the war, when threatened by a Negro on
his own plantation, Forrest shot the man. Other Negroes summoned a deputy
sheriff, who arrested Forrest and took him by boat to Memphis for court-martial
by the army of occupation. Federal soldiers on board recognized the Confederate
general, treated him to drinks, and urged him to debark with them. "But I have
given my word to Mr. Shaw," said Forrest. "And he is a gentleman. . . . We must
all get back to law sometime. I'll have to stand trial." The next day he was acquitted. Creekmore's typescript is a revised collation of material from many informants, some of it by other Federal Writers Project writers; I found no other
source for this episode (Record Group 60, Box 133, pp. 17–18, Mississippi State
Department of Archives and History).

(although his civilian role in the war was exemplary), "I know what's wrong: he's had to kill too many folks, and that's bad for a man" (260). But even the representative and teacher of the law, Judge Wilkins, fully expects Bayard to respond to his father's death by seeking out Redmond and shooting him. In fact the professor offers his young student his own pistol, repeating, nine years later, Uncle Buck McCaslin's gesture to Bayard. A few hours later the gesture is made again, this time by Drusilla, with Colonel Sartoris' pistols. And as Bayard crosses the square toward Redmond's office, Wyatt offers his. Only Bayard's Aunt Jenny will forgive him if he fails to seek out Redmond and shoot him.

A PRIESTESS OF REVENGE

Of all these pressures upon Bayard the most intense, most dire, and most difficult to resist is the "dark and passionate voracity," the "fierce exaltation" with which Drusilla in "An Odor of Verbena" seems transformed from the tomboy in "Raid" and the Drusilla returned from the war "working with Joby and Ringo and Father and me like another man" in "Skirmish at Sartoris" (270, 221). Faulkner's conception of Drusilla has been attributed by critics to a number of unlikely sources—*Orlando Furioso* (in which a character so named appears), *Hedda Gabler*, and Scott's *Rob Roy*, in each of which are fortuitous resemblances to some aspects of Drusilla Hawk's role in *The Unvanquished*.[20] In fact, however, Drusilla probably evolved from none of these presumed antecedents.

Her character is not presented consistently: in "Raid," as seen through the eyes of the fourteen-year-old Bayard, his twenty-year-old cousin Drusilla is realistically drawn. She appears already to have denied her own sexuality: "Her hair was cut short;

20. James E. Kibler, "A Possible Source in Ariosto for Drusilla," *Mississippi Quarterly*, XXIII (1970), 321–22; Edward L. Tucker, "Faulkner's Drusilla and Ibsen's Hedda," *Modern Drama*, XVI (1973), 157–61; Richard A. Milum, "Faulkner, Scott and Another Source for Drusilla," *Mississippi Quarterly*, XXXI (1976), 425–28.

it looked like Father's would" when his was cut "with a bayonet"; Drusilla "was sunburned and her hands hard and scratched like a man's that works" (103). Bayard, however, doesn't even think about this, accepting her hard-bitten appearance as the result of her having to do manual labor and live a hard life now that Hawkhurst is burned to the ground. It is Drusilla who tells of the race between the Confederate and Northern locomotives "like a meeting between two iron knights of the old time, not for material gain but for principle—honor denied with honor, courage denied with courage—the deed done not for the end but for the sake of the doing—put to the ultimate test and proving nothing save the finality of death and the vanity of all endeavor" (111). The pursuit by the Union engine of the one the Rebels had captured is thus a metaphor, in Drusilla's telling and in Bayard's remembering, for the entire Confederate enterprise, doomed but undertaken in a spirit of *sprezzatura*, as an expression of reckless courage, of character.

This is of course the ultimately romantic point of view, and Drusilla is a doomed romantic. Her fiancé had fallen in the Battle of Shiloh, she is a widow before being a bride, but instead of participating in the conventional Southern genteel sentimentality—widow's weeds, endless mourning, withdrawal from the world—she has turned the other face of her romantic illusions and, denying her femininity, is self-lacerating, cynical. Bayard observes that she cannot sleep. She replies:

Why not stay awake now? Who wants to sleep now, with so much happening, so much to see? Living used to be dull, you see. Stupid. You lived in the same house your father was born in, and your father's sons and daughters had the sons and daughters of the same Negro slaves to nurse and coddle; and then you grew up and you fell in love with your acceptable young man, and in time you would marry him, in your mother's wedding gown, perhaps, and with the same silver for presents she had received; and then you settled down forevermore while you got children to feed and bathe and dress until they grew up too. . . . Stupid, you see. But now you can see for yourself how it is; it's fine now; you don't have to worry about the house and silver, because they got burned up and carried away; and you don't have to worry about the negroes, because they tramp the roads all night waiting for a chance to drown in homemade Jordan; and you don't have to worry about getting children . . . because the young men can ride away and get killed in fine battles; and you don't even have to sleep alone, you don't even have to sleep at all.   (114–15)

And she begs Bayard to ask his father to let her join his regiment dressed as a common soldier. This in fact she does.

Thus far Drusilla has been drawn with psychological accuracy and empathy as a brave and resolute young woman deeply wounded by the loss of her father, her fiancé and her home. Her rejection of the Southern tradition of femininity is understandable; what she chooses in its place, however, is a course of conduct equally traditional, though opposed to the conventions she has abjured in her speech to Bayard. Drusilla as the disguised soldier and, later, as "the Greek amphora priestess of a succinct and formal revenge" (252) is a figure drawn from several traditional sources. The bereaved girl has been cast as the inversion of a popular convention and been mythologized in the extremity of her emotion and hysteria.

None of Faulkner's critics seems to have doubted that a young woman really could, by merely cutting her hair and wearing a uniform, join a troop of partisan rangers—men of the character described by General Sherman—without even a tent "bivouacking at night surrounded by sleeping men" (as her mother protests), and spend a couple of years chasing Yankees about the countryside untouched by any of her messmates. Drusilla might desex herself, but a reader's disbelief can be suspended only so far. Taken literally, her military service is preposterous; Drusilla the Female Soldier is a figure of pure fantasy: of literary fantasy and of folk fantasy.

The girl disguised as a youth is, of course, a stock property in romance. The plots of *As You Like It, Twelfth Night,* and *Cymbeline* require this disguise; it is a commonplace of popular literature in the nineteenth century. For instance, Faulkner's great-grandfather, Col. W. C. Falkner, in 1851 published a narrative poem based on his experience in the Mexican War. *The Siege of Monterey* has as frontispiece "a woodcut of a young woman in soldier's uniform on a field of battle." In the same year Colonel Falkner brought out a novel, *The Spanish Heroine.* "Like her predecessor the heroine donned a uniform and saved her lover (this time an American) during the battle of Monterey."[21] Colonel Falkner, or his descendant, may have derived this notion from a widespread folk tradition. In *American Balladry from British Broadsides*, G. Malcolm Laws lists thirteen ballads with the plot of girls disguised as soldiers or sailors collected in the South, one of them from Mississippi.[22]

Drusilla's service with the regiment differs, however, from that of the heroines of these ballads and romances. They, to a woman, have enlisted in order to rejoin their absent lovers. But Drusilla's lover is dead. "Can't you understand that I am tired of burying husbands in this war?" she replies to her mother's bewailing her disgracing herself, "[that] I am riding in Cousin John's troops not to find a man but to hurt Yankees?" (220). As the inversion of the popular tradition of the Disguised Soldier, Drusilla is on her way to becoming the mythologized avenging fury of the final pages. It is as though Faulkner, having summoned up the shade of his great-great-grandfather in the character of Colonel Sartoris, has summoned beside him Colonel Falkner's imagined heroine, the Disguised Soldier, not only to serve in his regiment but to become his bride in a sexless union. When Drusilla can no longer hold out against the ladies' sodality, Colonel Sartoris consoles her: "What's a dress? It don't matter. Come. Get up, soldier" (231). Obeying her commander, in this spirit, after the interruption of Colonel Sartoris' killing the carpetbaggers to prevent the fraudulent election, she marries him.

Four years later, Colonel Sartoris is no longer the dashing figure of romance who led his troops with such bravura and escaped from or captured regiments of Yankees with such derring-

---

21. Blotner, *Faulkner: A Biography*, I, 18.

22. G. Malcolm Laws, *American Balladry from British Broadsides* (Philadelphia, 1957), ballads N1–N10, N14, N15, N17; these have such titles as "The Female Sailor Bold," "The Female Warrior," "Disguised Sailor." In Arthur Palmer Hudson, *Folksongs of Mississippi and Their Background* (Chapel Hill, 1936), No. 34, "The Wars in Germany," is a version of Laws's N7, "Jack Monroe."

do. The war has taken a toll on him too: he has been hardened, inured to feeling. The habit of command and the need to act boldly prove attributes not so appropriate to peacetime life. Bayard's father is now completely preoccupied with his plan to rebuild a railroad, to rebuild the economy—Drusilla tells Bayard that "He is thinking of this whole country which he is trying to raise by its bootstraps," but she knows that "A dream is not a very safe thing to be near. . . . It's like a loaded pistol with a hair trigger; if it stays alive long enough, somebody is going to be hurt" (256, 257). Bayard observes his father's domineering intractability in the colonel's gratuitous quarrel with his sometime partner Redmond.

For Drusilla, love of death has displaced love itself. When Bayard repeats to her George Wyatt's cautionary remark that the colonel's problem is having killed "too many folks," and that he ought to ease up on Redmond, not make "a brave man that made one mistake eat crow all the time," she admonishes him:

"There are worse things than killing men, Bayard. There are worse things than being killed. Sometimes I think the finest thing that can happen to a man is to love someone, a woman preferably, well, hard hard hard, then to die young because he believed what he could not help but believe and was what he could not (could not? would not) help but be." Now she was looking at me in a way she never had before . . . the scent of the verbena in her hair seemed to have increased a hundred times . . . to be everywhere in the dusk in which something was about to happen which I had never dreamed of. Then she spoke. "Kiss me, Bayard."   (261–62)

Some have opined that Drusilla has no incestuous feelings for Bayard, although he, out of respect and love for his father, instinctively feels the impropriety of her request. Drusilla will not accept a stiff, token kiss, so he embraces her. "Then she came to me, melted as women will and can . . . using the wrists to hold my face to hers until there was no need for the wrists; I thought then of the woman of thirty, the symbol of the ancient and eternal Snake" (262). After this impassioned embrace Drusilla removes the sprig of verbena from her hair and puts it in Bayard's lapel. What can this mean but that she foresees the "something"

that "was about to happen which [he] had never dreamed of"—
the probability that her husband would provoke Redmond too
far and might be killed, and the certainty, as she feels it to be,
that Bayard, whom she has just reminded of his part in Grumby's
death, would reenact that part on behalf of his murdered father.
It is this vision of Bayard, whether as successful avenger or as
cut down in the attempt, which arouses the latent sexuality of
his stepmother who is also his cousin and only six years older
than he.

When Bayard, honor bound, says he must tell his father what
has happened, Drusilla replies: "Yes, you must tell him. Kiss
me." And they embrace again "like it had been before. No. Twice,
a thousand times and never like" (263–64). At dinner that night,
"Drusilla . . . talked with a sort of feverish and glittering volu-
bility" (265). But when Bayard does tell his father, his revelation
elicits no response at all. "It was worse with him than not hearing: it didn't even matter" (266). Sartoris is too preoccupied to
attend to his son's having embraced his wife; with Bayard's legal
training, the colonel tells him, he can soon take part in the family enterprise, the railroad: "Yes. I have accomplished my aim,
and now I shall do a little moral housecleaning. I am tired of killing men, no matter what the necessity nor the end. Tomorrow,
when I go to town and meet Ben Redmond, I shall be unarmed"
(266). Now we know why Drusilla has suddenly turned to Bayard
as an object of desire. For she must have known that John Sartoris
wishes to renounce violence and killing—her husband would
likely have said as much to her before telling his son. And she
knows that, unarmed, he may be killed. A peacemaker has no
appeal to Drusilla's imagination, for the grief, the renunciations
of six years have fixated her in her desire, her need, for an avenger.

When Sartoris does call upon Redmond, it is too late for his
own "moral housecleaning"; having been provoked beyond endurance, Redmond kills him.[23] And when Judge Wilkins flings

23. Evidently not the next day, for Bayard is studying his Coke, at the university forty miles away, when Ringo rides to fetch him. Nor did Sartoris go to Redmond unarmed; "John had the derringer inside his cuff like always, but he never
touched it, never made a move toward it," Wyatt tells Bayard (268).

open the door of his room without knocking, Bayard instinctively knows what has happened and that now, in the style of the Scottish clans, he is "The Sartoris." Arriving home, Bayard looks at his father's body, "just as I had imagined it—sabre, plumes, and all . . . the empty hands still now beneath the invisible stain of what had been (once, surely) needless blood" (272). Drusilla, "the scent of the verbena in her hair," holds out to him his father's duelling pistols: "'Take them, Bayard,' she said, in the same tone in which she had said 'kiss me' last summer . . . watching me with that passionate and voracious exaltation, speaking in a voice fainting and passionate with promise: 'Take them. I have kept them for you. . . . Do you feel them? the long true barrels true as justice, the triggers (you have fired them) quick as retribution, the two of them slender and invisible and fatal as the physical shape of love?'" (273). Then, removing the sprig of verbena from her hair, "I abjure verbena forever more; I have smelled it above the odor of courage; that was all I wanted," and she places it in his lapel. In an ecstasy of expectation Drusilla goes on: "How beautiful you are: do you know it? How beautiful: Young, to be permitted to kill, to be permitted vengeance, to take into your bare hands the fire of heaven that cast down Lucifer. No; I. I gave it to you; I put it into your hands." Bayard recalls, "She had taken my right hand which still held one of the pistols . . . and kissed it before I comprehended why she took it" (274).

This woman in her exaltation at the prospect of another death Bayard had described, anticipating her response, as "the Greek amphora priestess of a succinct and formal violence" (252). This image presents her at once as the acolyte of a primitive, divinely sanctioned, ritualistic revenge and as a figure on a vase, similar to Faulkner's favorite and often-invoked "Ode on a Grecian Urn." Indeed Drusilla is "half in love with easeful death," but she is no "unravished bride of quietude," this mad priestess of unforgiving vengeance. Like Keats's bride, however, she is forever fixed in her one attitude, perfected, incapable of responding to the changes and vicissitudes of our life. Upon her realization that Bayard does not intend to kill Redmond, she succumbs to hysteria. "I kissed his hand!" she whispers aghast, "beginning to laugh, the laughter rising, becoming a scream . . . the laughter spilling between her fingers like vomit, the incredulous betrayed eyes still matching" (275), until Aunt Jenny has her led away.

Now Bayard is alone with his decision. What neither Drusilla nor Wyatt realizes is that in renouncing revenge he is in fact fulfilling the wish of his father, who hoped, after so much killing, to cleanse his conscience and did not draw his derringer when facing Redmond's pistol. Only Aunt Jenny—whose situation is nearly identical to Drusilla's, having lost her husband of two weeks at the very start of the war—understands. She will accept Bayard, love him, "Even if you spend the day hidden in the stable loft" (280). She knows Drusilla to be "a poor hysterical young woman" and knows that Bayard is not afraid (276). Bidding him good night, she calls him "son," assuming the role—though she is only Drusilla's age—of Bayard's mother.

The next morning as Bayard rides to town, Ringo, Wyatt, and his father's troopers gathered in the square all exert upon him the community's pressure for vengeance. Bayard declines Wyatt's offer to go with him. "I walked steadily on enclosed in the now fierce odor of the verbena sprig . . . walked steadily toward him . . . in a dreamlike state in which there was neither time nor distance" (285–86). Redmond awaits him, pistol on his desk. But he, too, has had enough of killing and, seeing that Bayard is unarmed, fires aslant. Bayard remembers "the sudden orange bloom and smoke . . . as they had appeared against Grumby's greasy Confederate coat" but "I knew it was not aimed at me" (286–87). A brave man, Redmond too has fulfilled his part in the necessary ritual; now he walks in silence through the men waiting outside and boards the outgoing train, never to be seen in Jefferson again. The men rush inside: "You walked in here without even a pocket knife and let him miss you twice. My god in heaven," Wyatt exclaims, then sends word at once to "tell his folks it's all over and he's all right" (288). To Bayard he says: "I wouldn't have done it that way, myself. . . . But that's your way or you wouldn't have done it." Bayard's courage requires admiration. "Well, by God, maybe you're right, maybe there's been enough killing in your family" (289).

Bayard rides home with Ringo; when they come to the creek bottom where years before they "had built the pen to hide the Yankee mules," they dismount, and Bayard, exhausted from the tension of his ordeal, falls into a deep sleep from which he awakens "crying, crying too hard to stop it" (290). (The only other time he had cried was after tying Grumby's hand to the headboard of Granny Millard's grave.) When he arrives at Sartoris, Aunt Jenny tells him that Drusilla has left on the evening train, gone to live with her brother. The amphora priestess has no role at Sartoris now. But, on the pillow of his bed she has left a single sprig of verbena, filling the room, the dusk, the evening with the odor that she said "you could smell above the smell of horses and courage and so it was the only one that was worth the wearing" (253–54).

We are given no comment from Uncle Buck McCaslin this time, but in effect the community has joined in saying "Ain't I told you he is John Sartoris' boy?" For Bayard has won their respect, even Drusilla's, by not backing down from the challenge which he does not accept. Yet again, he does accept that he must observe the punctiliousness of the code duello in showing himself to his adversary. But he does this in a gesture not of forgiveness but of transcending the code he is at the same time observing. Recognizing this, Redmond, who, we are told, is no coward, fires the obligatory shots, aimed off target. The forms have been observed though their function is acknowledged to be obsolete. Thus Bayard outgrows the brutality and savagery of the war, and enters his manhood as one who has been tested and has passed his test.

BLACK AND WHITE

"I have a series of six stories about a white boy and a negro boy during the civil war. . . . What do you think about getting them out as a book?" Faulkner wrote to Bennett Cerf on 28 December 1936. He had not yet written "An Odor of Verbena," would not until the following July; in his always-urgent need for an advance he presented the magazine versions of the first six tales as a prospective book.[24] But "An Odor of Verbena" went much more deeply into Faulkner's themes than had the earlier tales, except for "Vendée"; when he revised the magazine texts he enriched them. What had begun as a series of adventure tales about a white and a Negro boy became a much more complex work.

Its initial impulse, however, runs through the first five chapters. (Ringo does not play a role in "Skirmish at Sartoris," Faulkner's social comedy of Aunt Louisa's forcing her daughter Drusilla to marry her C.O.) From Bayard's infancy he and Ringo were inseparable: "Ringo and I had been born in the same month and had both fed at the same breast and had slept together and eaten together for so long that Ringo called Granny 'Granny' just like I did, until maybe he wasn't a nigger anymore or maybe I wasn't a white boy anymore, the two of us neither, not even people any longer: the two supreme undefeated like two moths, two feathers riding above a hurricane" (7–8). All this eloquence to explain why the two took turns at being General Grant and General Pemberton while playing at war when twelve years old! What is suggested, here and throughout, is that the relationship of the two boys is not only close, not only symbiotic, but a twinning, a doubling of Bayard into his black mirror image, presented—uniquely in Faulkner's work—without tinge of guilt. There is not the slightest suspicion that Ringo is a by-blow of the colonel's; it's simply that the two age-mates have been constant companions, have done all they have done in each other's company.

And yet, despite this protestation of equality, Bayard says, "The arrangement was that I would be General Pemberton twice in succession and Ringo would be Grant, then I would have to be Grant once so Ringo could be General Pemberton or he wouldn't

---

24. Blotner, *Faulkner: A Biography,* II, 951; Blotner (ed.), *Selected Letters of William Faulkner* (New York, 1977), 100.

play anymore" (7). Even in this idealized relationship, color and status cannot be completely obliterated. But in *The Unvanquished* we come closer than anywhere else in Faulkner's work to their being ignored.

Compared to the other Negroes on the Sartoris place, Ringo enjoys many privileges. Evidently little work is required of him as it is of Joby, Loosh, and Louvinia. The blacks seem to be well treated and on the whole content and loyal to both the Sartoris family and, by extension, the Confederacy, except for Loosh, who defiantly proclaims himself liberated and betrays to the Yankees the whereabouts of the family silver, recently buried in the yard. "I don't belong to John Sartoris now; I belongs to me and God," Loosh declares (85). When Granny Millard responds: "But the silver belongs to John Sartoris. Who are you to give it away?" Loosh replies in a burst of eloquence as near as Faulkner comes to presenting the slaves' view of their situation, "You ax me that? . . . Where John Sartoris? Whyn't he come and ax me that? Let God ax John Sartoris who the man name that give me to him. Let the man that buried me in the black dark ax that of the man what dug me free" (85).

But freedom proves an illusion. Hundreds of slaves like Loosh have taken literally the Emancipation Proclamation and, ignorant and confused as they are, have mingled it with their religion's promise of deliverance. Through the night they march toward the river on the Alabama line, chanting and singing, the weaker ones falling by the way. On their visit to Hawkhurst, Granny Millard and the boys see these poor folk, hear their voices in the night. Granny tries to help one woman straggler, but what can she do? Drusilla, too, shows concern for their plight. But the Union Army, bringer of their liberation, has no succor to offer them, neither food, shelter, nor work, and in desperation the troops blow up the bridge across the river. No one takes responsibility for these Negroes set free by a proclamation in Washington. Granny persuades those who are foisted on her to return to their homes, though many of the homes have been razed by the invaders. Faulkner's view of emancipation is highly critical. A population of uneducated field hands has been told it is free, but the abrogation of the legal and social ties that held the society of the South together has been accompanied by no new arrangements to provide for these people unfitted to fend for themselves. The spectacle of crowds of Negroes marching, entranced in futility, to "a homemade Jordan" (as Drusilla calls it) signifies the collapse of social order. Conquest brings chaos. After a while Loosh gives up on being liberated and returns to Sartoris. There is nowhere else for him to go.

Ringo in no way identifies his own lot with that of Loosh or the marchers to Jordan. When Granny is put in charge of 110 Negroes, Ringo naturally assumes a proprietary air, helping decide how to manage them as well as the mules. He identifies himself completely with Granny Millard and Bayard, and, as is his wont, shows initiative, takes charge. For Ringo is a tad smarter than Bayard, the first to comprehend what's going on or being said, the first to speak up (as when he blurts that they are hunting Ab Snopes as well as Grumby); and Ringo it is who is so adept at forging requisitions and at drawing pictures of the destroyed Sartoris mansion. These evidences of Ringo's superior acuity were introduced when Faulkner rewrote his magazine stories to make them into a novel. The stories were originally written to be sold, as their author's correspondence tells us, and of course Faulkner knew there was no way in 1936 that he could sell *The Saturday Evening Post* a string of tales in which a black boy is smarter than the heir to a plantation. But the material revised for a book was something else again.

At the time that Faulkner was writing and revising these stories, he was also wrestling with the manuscript first called "Dark House," later retitled "Absalom, Absalom!" The parallel has been often remarked between Bayard and Ringo's return together from Jefferson to Sartoris when Bayard is summoned to avenge his father's murder, and Henry Sutpen and Charles Bon's riding together toward Sutpen's Hundred, where Henry is determined to prevent Charles, his octoroon half-brother, from marrying their sister Judith, thus from committing both incest and miscegenation. It is as though in simultaneously, or alternately, imagining the anguish of Henry and Charles and the guilt-free relationship of Bayard and Ringo, Faulkner was freeing his imagination of the burdens of Sutpen's dark house. For the two boys in *The Unvanquished* act with single impulse and single will. Ringo doesn't think twice about assuming that he, too, will avenge Granny Millard's murder, nor does Bayard for a moment doubt that Ringo will come along. In the event, they *both* kill Grumby, Ringo with his knife, Bayard with Buck McCaslin's pistol; as they both endured the privations of the two-month pursuit, both experience the horror of their grisly revenge and the release of tears at its accomplishment.

In "An Odor of Verbena," however, ten years have passed, and they are twenty-four. Bayard prepares for man's estate by studying law at the University, but what estate can Ringo prepare for? He is now relegated to being merely a servant whom Bayard refers to as "my boy," the faithful and resourceful one who rides forty miles into the night to summon Bayard to his father's funeral, having paused only to arrange a fresh horse for his return. Bayard knows that he can never be "The Sartoris" to Ringo, with "his outrageous assurance gained from too long and too close association with white people" (248, 250). On the homeward ride these are their only words:

> "We could bushwhack him," he said. "Like we done Grumby that day. But I reckon that wouldn't suit that white skin you walks around in."
> "No," I said.   (251)

It has been objected that Bayard didn't bushwhack Grumby, Grumby bushwhacked Granny; but Ringo in fact had bushwhacked Grumby, leaping upon him with a pocketknife in his hand. That was as close as Ringo could come to observing the code duello, in its least courtly form. This time, too, Ringo feels it is proper for him to participate in the expected ritual. He says, "I'm going with you," as Bayard reaches the square the next morning, and Bayard sees the bulge inside Ringo's shirt of the pistol they had taken from Grumby (283). Everybody wants to give Bayard a gun. Ringo's response to the situation is just like everyone else's, except Bayard's.

Some readers have found in Ringo's expectation that the colonel's murder will be avenged evidence of his lack of moral growth—he is, morally, still fifteen. In truth, he is like the white folks all around him; who, besides Bayard, has an inkling that the way to deal with Redmond is anything other than to drill him with a pistol? In his study of Faulkner's handling of black characters Lee Jenkins suggests that "the distinguishing characteristic of [Ringo's] similarity to the whites, and the basis of Faulkner's presentation of his emotional attachment to the whites is his intelligence. . . . Ringo's intelligence assures him that the only way to get on is through identifying with whiteness; or it may be that the fact that he has intelligence would *mean* that he would identify with whiteness. Being intelligent, he cannot, therefore, be black, or use that intelligence in the interest of blacks—which means, therefore, in his own interest."[25] Ringo, then, is caught in a tragic dilemma, for his identity, his own self-image, depends upon the continuation of the status quo of Southern white society. In a world in which the marchers to Jordan are truly freed, what would Ringo be? If Bayard achieves moral transcendence, Ringo remains entailed in his emotional commitment to the ancien régime; but by the end of *The Unvanquished* that regime has been overthrown, and the implication is heavy that Ringo will be a man displaced by history. Perhaps Faulkner had for his character the affection many a reader feels, and so could take no joy in further exploring Ringo's sad prospects. Unlike most of Faulkner's characters, who reappear in novel after novel, Ringo is seen only in this one. He could participate in Bayard's boyhood and initiation, but could not share the manhood of a transcendent morality into which Bayard has been initiated.

Counterpoised to the Northern alternatives to slavery—the Union Army's lack of responsibility to the emancipated Negroes, the carpetbaggers' running the election of an illiterate for-

25. Lee Jenkins, *Faulkner and Black-White Relations: A Psychoanalytic Approach* (New York, 1981), 127.

mer Benbow family coachman as marshal—Faulkner gives us a Southern alternative which, he seems to say, had it been given an opportunity by history to be tried, could have remedied the fatal flaw in Southern society. This passage, which Faulkner inserted in *The Unvanquished* when revising his short stories, interrupts the action (in "Retreat") as Rosa Millard and the boys prepare to leave Sartoris for Memphis. "Uncle Buck McCaslin came hobbling across the square," and here follows a six-page disquisition on Uncle Buck and his brother Uncle Buddy's manner of treating the McCaslin Negroes, and their relationship to Colonel Sartoris and his regiment (54).

Moved by what we do not yet know, the McCaslins no longer live in their big house built by slave labor; ever since their father's death, they have "lived in a two-room log house with about a dozen dogs, and they kept their niggers in the manor house." Every night the bachelors "would drive them into the house and lock the door" while the blacks "escaped out the back" (52–53). This observance of a form no longer functional "was like a game with rules"—it was agreed the brothers were not to see the nightly escapes. The only clue to this strange business is that it did not start until the elder McCaslin died; not until "The Bear" in *Go Down, Moses* do we learn why the eccentric uncles play this "game" with their blacks, or why, in *The Unvanquished*, they had "ideas about social relationship that maybe fifty years after they were both dead people would have a name for. . . . They believed that land did not belong to people but that people belonged to land" (54). And they worked out a system "by which all their niggers were to be freed, not given freedom, but earning it, buying it not in money from Uncle Buck and Buddy, but in work from the plantation" (54). What is more, they had further "ideas about men and land," populist ideas by which poor whites were "to pool their little patches of poor hill land along with the niggers and the McCaslin plantation," comprising a sort of farmers' cooperative so successful that these "white trash" farmers "looked on Uncle Buck and Buddy like Deity Himself" (55).

These measures, we will learn in "The Bear," are motivated by the brothers' effort to expiate their guilt for owning land, slaves, and incestuously begotten half-black kinsmen, guilt inherited from their father. Here it is strongly implied that the McCaslins, "ahead of their time," had pragmatically worked out ways by which the slaves earned their freedom rather than receiving it as an empty gift, and had devised an economically sound solution to the endemic poverty of the poor white underclass, a solution which did not require the dismantling of the plantation system and the displacement of the squierarchy. The McCaslins' Southern solutions to and expiations of the problems and sins of the South, however, are scarcely to be taken seriously as options the South might have chosen, for the uncles and their notions are presented as quite eccentric in the view of everyone around them. At the same time, if we can accept such homegrown backcountry reformers as Uncle Buck and Uncle Buddy, we must take them at their own measure, including in their character their high-spirited recklessness, their spirit of gamesmanship, their prowess at poker, Uncle Buck's fierce loyalty to his ex-commander John Sartoris, his tenacity in leading the boys to Grumby, his bloody-mindedness in telling Bayard what he must do to Grumby so that Rosa Millard can rest quiet in her grave. All this detail, with its unrevealed motivation, suggests that even while writing *The Unvanquished* Faulkner already had in mind the McCaslin saga to be embodied several years later in *Go Down, Moses.*

We know that Faulkner often conceived of episodes, characters, whole novels of his interlinked county saga achronologically, commencing the Sartoris history, in *Flags in the Dust* (and *Sartoris*) with Bayard—a boy in *The Unvanquished*—as a querulous old man. Although in *Father Abraham* Faulkner outlined the arrival of Flem Snopes in Frenchman's Bend, not until eight years later did he provide a story for Flem's barn-burning father Ab, and he would leave unfinished the whole saga of the descent of the Snopeses upon Yoknapatawpha County until he revised and greatly expanded and improved the "Father

Abraham" manuscript between 1938 and 1940, bringing these revisions together in his most sustained and perfected comic novel, *The Hamlet*—the comedy, as always in Faulkner, poised against the tragic knowledge folk laughter makes it possible for us to bear.

III

The Hamlet

THE MATTER OF SNOPES

On July 17, 1842, the *Mississippi Creole* of Canton, Mississippi, published a story bound to interest its readers:

DIAMOND CUT DIAMOND

A Yankee pedlar, one of the great tribe who have learned the art of skinning a flint, and of drawing blood out of a stone, entered the store of a Yankee merchant, and wanted to sell him some razor strops. The merchant declining to have anything to do with him ordered him out. A Yankee pedlar is not got off so easily. There is no getting rid of him while there is a chance of his wearying your patience, until you make a purchase. He's like the immortal "Jim Baggs." He knows the value of peace, and questions, and won't leave his noise unless he is well paid for it.

"Come, mister, now I swow I must trade with you."

"You'll do nothing of the kind."

"Look here now—I'll take any good you've got in payment."

"No you won't."

"O get out. I tell you what I'll do, Mister, I'll sell these strops at the lowest wholesale prices, and take any of your goods at your retail figure. That's fair."

"Well, as you're so pressing, I'll take twelve dozen at $6 per dozen, that will be $72, which you shall take out in any goods I choose, that I have here in the store."

"Well, I guess you ain't got nothing here that I can't dispose of somewhere."

"Make out your bill and receipt it."

The pedlar did so, and called on the merchant to select the goods he chose to pay him in, whereupon the merchant handed him six dozen back, and said, "I retail these at one dollar each—we are now square—I

71

bought them at your wholesale price, and I sell them to you again at my retail price."

The pedlar looked daggers, but he had to put up with the mortification of being overreached, which was his greatest trouble, and made him downright savage.[1]

This yarn of the Yankee peddler as the trickster tricked, long familiar in New England, had made its way, through newspaper exchange columns and doubtless by word of mouth as well, to antebellum Mississippi. The same trick is told as played by a merchant in Providence, R.I., on a peddler of brooms; it was a staple in the large repertoire of mercantile jokelore.[2] It is the paradigm Faulkner elaborates and expands in *The Hamlet*, in his usual fashion embedding an abstract and archetypal plot motif in a richly realized matrix of character and milieu.

Identifying with the landed gentry in the country and the professional class in the town, Faulkner has a simultaneous aversion to and fascination with the intricate operations of the mercantile mind. His diagnosis of the fateful inner flaw of Southern society identifies it not alone with the inherited liabilities of the squierarchs who were responsible for slavery and its attendant evils, nor with the Northerners who invaded, conquered, and despoiled the South and during Reconstruction governed the region with a horde of carpetbaggers. No, the inner decay of Southern society Faulkner attributes to the rise of a class of native Southerners, the redneck entrepreneurs who, with neither inherited culture, fidelity to religion, nor the moral scruples produced by refinement of living, swarmed over the South like locusts, insinuating themselves into the operations of society, displacing men of finer character. These were the bushwhackers who evaded Confederate service during the Civil War and preyed upon the women, children, and blacks left defenseless by the departure in the army of their husbands, fathers, and masters.

1. *Mississippi Creole*, July 17, 1842, in Record Group 60, Box 121, Federal Writers Project Files, Mississippi State Department of Archives and History, Jackson.

2. I quote this yarn and discuss the motif in *Form and Fable in American Fiction* (New York, 1961), 50.

Their descendants were a rabble of unscrupulous poor white trash who, by wiles, trickery, deceits, succeeded in dominating the established institutions—the banks, the political structure. In *The Hamlet* Flem Snopes arrives in Frenchman's Bend and works his way through and upward, first in that crossroads settlement, then, in two later novels (*The Town* and *The Mansion*), in Jefferson, the county seat. He is the son of Ab Snopes, who betrayed Rosa Millard in *The Unvanquished.*

Flem is the most developed treatment of the Yankee peddler's ethos in our literature. In him the Yankee love of trading becomes a lust for moneymaking and a compulsion to dominate others. Flem has no other ambition, no other emotion, but to get the better of everyone else by outsharping them in his deals, thereby moving upward in society himself and bringing in his train his tribe of nasty cousins. Flem's forebears are Haliburton's Sam Slick, Hawthorne's genial Domenicus Pike, and, more directly, Johnson Jones Hooper's Simon Suggs, whose motto was "IT IS GOOD TO BE SHIFTY IN A NEW COUNTRY." Flem is Faulkner's early twentieth-century version of Melville's Confidence-Man, with similar hints of supernatural and demoniacal character. Like the Confidence-Man, Flem is a rapacious entrapper of souls.

In the jokelore exemplified by the peddler and the merchant, and their exchange of razor strops or brooms, the point was that they traded for the sake of trading in a competition to see who got the better end of the bargain. Usually in these folk fables the resentment of his victims against the itinerant Yankee—an outlander as well as a sharper—is dramatized by giving the victory to the merchant, who, after all, is rooted in the community where the joke was told. Faulkner appropriates the dynamics of this contest of mercantile virtuosity while, in his typical fashion, reversing the theme of the tale in a couple of ways. In the folktale the only thing that makes the merchant worthier of victory is his not being a travelling Yankee; otherwise, in acuity, in mercantile ethics, he is indistinguishable from his adversary. As far as I know, no one before Faulkner ever had the notion not only of making the storekeeper the heartless villain who will go to any lengths to put over a deal but of making his adversary, the peddler, a man of good heart, of sweet character—the store-keeper's worthy rival when it comes to seeing through a stacked deal but who, in the interactions between them, provides a moral center. Such is the reversal of roles Faulkner works out in the rivalry between Flem Snopes and the travelling sewing-machine agent V. K. Ratliff, through whose consciousness we are privy to much of the plot and by whose standards we are enabled to measure the depravity of Flem and his tribe.

It is really remarkable that as early as 1926 Faulkner had Flem's character and machinations already in mind in such de-tail, though to be sure the sewing-machine agent is scarcely developed in the unfinished sketch "Father Abraham." These pages originally bore the title (from Balzac) "The Peasants," and clearly reflect long discussions with Faulkner's early mentor, Phil Stone, the Yale-educated lawyer a few years his senior who had introduced Faulkner to French Symbolist poetry and to such authors otherwise unread in Oxford as Conrad and Joyce.

Years later, Stone evidently felt he had received insufficient credit—from Faulkner himself as well as from his admiring critics—as the distance widened between the one-time men-tor and his former protégé. Stone made some rather grasping claims, writing to one correspondent in 1950, "I actually made [Faulkner's] humor for him. At the beginning he was a very humorless person." And, to another in 1957, "Just when the Snopes idea was first propounded I cannot tell you except that it was some time in the 20s before *Sartoris* was written. The idea was mine, as were a great number of the incidents. . . . The core of the Snopes legend was an idea I gave Bill . . . and it was . . . that the real revolution in the South was not the race situation but the rise of the rednecks who did not have any of the scruples of the old aristocracy, to places of power and wealth."[3] The rise of rednecks like Senators Vardaman and Bilbo and, closer at hand, local politicians and bankers was clearly a threat to the

3. Phil Stone to Glenn O. Carey, February 9, 1950, in Louis Daniel Brodsky and Robert W. Hamblin (eds.), *Faulkner: A Comprehensive Guide to the Brodsky Collection* (Jackson, Miss., 1984), 50; Stone to James Meriwether, February 19, 1957, *ibid.*, 207.

position of both their families; Stone's father and Faulkner's grandfather were presidents of the two banks in Oxford, and they had seen these eminent gentlemen shouldered aside by ruthless arrivistes. Stone encouraged Faulkner to dramatize and satirize the upward mobility of those wrong people; and since "the Snopes legend" gives sardonic embodiment not merely of Mississippi foibles but of the corruption of American life, Faulkner's elaboration of what had begun as jokes between him and Stone became in time a novel worthy of comparison to Melville's and Mark Twain's desperate satires on "the damned human race."

Twenty years after those conversations with Faulkner, Stone seemed unable to distinguish between an "idea" for a fiction and the fiction developed from his suggestions. Although he defined his own role in Faulkner's work by saying that "actually I never wrote a line of Bill's books. I simply listened to the manuscripts he read, suggested changes and furnished him with a number of characters and incidents," Stone came to resent Faulkner's great success, and in this same letter he put down his former friend as merely "one of the best second-rate writers of fiction. . . . [H]e very obviously does not care for my company and I don't know of anything that suits me better." Yet Faulkner felt that Stone deserved to be the dedicatee of *The Town.* In the same year as this letter in which Stone called it "ironical . . . that Bill got the Nobel Prize [in 1950] for nothing he had written after 1940 and it would not surprise me if he did not play out entirely as a writer,"[4] Faulkner inscribed the second volume of his Snopes trilogy

> To PHIL STONE
> *He did half the laughing for thirty years*

However much of the original donnée for the Snopes saga derived from Stone, over the next fifteen years Faulkner had great difficulty developing the promising material beyond the "Father Abraham" manuscript. This fragment, it will be recalled, re-

---

4. Stone to Meriwether, February 19, 1957, *ibid.,* 208.

counts Flem's arrival at Uncle Billy Varner's store, quickly mentions his marriage to Eula Varner, their departure for Texas, and then moves to the auction of the spotted horses on Flem's return a year later. Ratliff (in *Father Abraham* he is called Suratt, changed by Faulkner because there was an Oxford family by that name) is not the narrator, as he is of much of the action in *The Hamlet*. Suratt is not even introduced until page 29, where he is mentioned merely as "a sewing-machine agent," and he does not reappear until page 56, where his name is first given; but from page 63 on, he becomes the central figure. He deprecates the horses, then gets I. O. Snopes to admit that they are owned by Flem. But a few pages later *Father Abraham* breaks off abruptly with the sentence, "Suratt's buckboard stood at the hitching rail." Having introduced Suratt toward the end of his fragment, Faulkner was becoming aware of how useful this character might be in his chronicle of Snopesism. But it took him over fifteen years to figure out what to do with him.

The widening rift between Faulkner and Phil Stone may be linked to Faulkner's difficulty in developing the Matter of Snopes. From his correspondence it is clear that Stone never changed his ideas about rednecks an iota from the censoriousness behind the satire he and Bill Faulkner laughed at together back in the 1920s. But meanwhile Faulkner, with greater sympathy during the Depression for the rural poor, wrote *As I Lay Dying* (1930), in which he empathized with and entered the consciousness of a whole family of dirt-poor rednecks, and *Light in August* (1932), with its understanding portrayal of an outcast half-black murderer, a simple, poor mill hand, and a pregnant yet innocent country girl. Brooding upon the Snopeses, Faulkner found he did not wish to treat every last one of them with contemptuous satire, as Phil Stone doubtless advised. Faulkner, with his sensibility so subversive of establishment pieties, would in time imagine himself inside the stunted, warped soul of a mean little two-penny Ahab like Mink Snopes and create his character with sympathy and understanding; he would portray at least one Snopes, Eck, who can feel pity; and he would imagine an idiot, Ike Snopes, in love with a cow, but far from judging this descent into animal husbandry as merely comical-despicable, Faulkner presents it in a *tour de force* of lyrical romanticism. Faulkner's view of his imagined world and its inhabitants was far wider than that of even his best-educated and most literate neighbor.

Yet on the level of gross caricature the Snopes legend offered a range of grotesque, perverse characters, the errata of mankind. In *Flags in the Dust* (written in 1926), Faulkner needed a character embodying the humor (in the medieval sense) of lust, and who better than a Snopes—so we meet Byron Snopes, bank teller and author of the anonymous pornographic letters he dictates to a boy, so they won't be traced by his own handwriting, and sends to Narcissa Benbow. In *The Town*, thirty years later, Faulkner will endow another Snopes, Montgomery Ward, with a similar penchant; for Monty Snopes, like his great-uncle Ab in the Civil War a hang-back from the draft, goes overseas in World War I to help Horace Benbow run the YMCA canteen and of course returns with a case of filthy pictures with which he sets up in the pornography business. The nomenclature of many Snopeses suggests the monodimensional nature of their characterization: who could take seriously as rounded human beings the aforementioned Montgomery Ward Snopes, or Eck's sons Wallstreet Panic and Admiral Dewey, or such other Snopes relations as Watkins Products, Orestes, and Launcelot (nicknamed Lump)? These are names out of the funny papers, good for single gags. In *Sanctuary* and *The Town*, how better portray a scheming, dealing, unsavory redneck politician than by having Clarence Snopes be a state senator? Along the lines of the tall tale tradition that glorified ugliness, Faulkner elaborates these numerous Snopeses; this tradition is evident in the names of the major Snopeses, Flem and Mink. Another tall tale tradition is illustrated by the visit, in *Sanctuary*, of Virgil Snopes and Fonzo to Miss Reba's brothel, the country boys thinking for two weeks that they are staying in a hotel.

Among the most memorable of these comic stereotypes is the pedant I. O. Snopes. His name suggests a torn, therefore worthless, promissory note. I. O. is defined in the Dickensian manner by one characteristic—his mouth is forever filled with proverbs, the wisdom of which is self-contradictory; appropriately so, since I. O. is a low-spirited bubblehead, adept at nothing, whose only skill is mean self-advancement. Faulkner's ultimate source for this avatar of folk wisdom is probably Sancho Panza, though he may well have been helped in his conception of I. O. by the appearance, in 1937, of Carl Sandburg's *The People, Yes.* In another connection I have observed of this work, with its lyrical-portentous populism, that "Some of its sections read like the published proverb collections of the American Dialect Society." A century and a half ago—on Tuesday, October 30, 1838—such a list of proverbs amused readers of the *Southern Argus* in Columbus, Mississippi:

A white glove often conceals a dirty hand. The remedy for injuries is not to remember them. Be a friend to yourself and others will. Go into the country to hear the news of town. Be not a baker if your head is made of butter. Call me cousin but cozen me not. Faint praise leads to disparagement. Ask thy purse what thou shouldst buy. Zeal without knowledge is like fire without light. . . . Beware of a silent dog and a wet rat.[5]

The string of non sequiturs, each a distillation of conventional wisdom, cannot help but be faintly amusing. The effect is intensified when, as in *The Hamlet,* a character utters proverbs in this disconnected manner, for our expectation is strong of consecutive discourse as a governing structure for conversation. Jack Houston has brought his horse to be shod and finds that Frenchman's Bend has a new blacksmith: "'Morning, morning,' he said, his bright little eyes darting. 'Want that horse shod, hey? Good, good: save the hoof and save all. Good-looking animal. Seen a considerable better one in a field a piece back. But no matter: love me, love my horse, beggars cant be choosers, if wishes was horseflesh we'd all own thoroughbreds'"[6] I. O. goes on like this—"'It's the old shop, the old stand; just a new broom

5. *Paul Bunyan, Last of the Frontier Demigods* (Philadelphia, 1952; rpr. Lincoln, Nebr., 1983), 134; Elizabeth Delby (comp.), "Proverbs," Federal Writers Project Files, Mississippi State Department of Archives and History.

6. Faulkner, *The Hamlet* (1940; rpr. New York, 1956), 65. Pagination hereafter will be indicated parenthetically in the text.

in it . . . give a dog a good name and you dont need to hang him' . . . his voice voluble and rapid and meaningless like something talking to itself about nothing in a deserted cavern" (63–65). Inevitably, in Flem's design, Cousin I. O., having failed at blacksmithing, replaces the village schoolmaster. And it is inevitable, in Faulkner's design, that the cant phrases of popular wisdom be put in the mouth of a self-serving fool.

The problem of how the materials in *Father Abraham* could be expanded into a longer work involves the point of view from which Flem, his machinations, and his dreadful family are perceived. In *Father Abraham* the authorial voice is detached and ironical; at some point Faulkner realized that using V. K. Suratt, or Ratliff, as a participant, as point of view, and as center of judgment upon the Snopeses, could open up the themes that had proved recalcitrant theretofore.

From the start Ratliff (I shall drop Suratt, as Faulkner did) had been imagined as a sewing-machine agent, that is, a travelling salesman—the modern equivalent of the nineteenth-century peddler. But why a salesman of sewing machines? Traditionally, peddlers hawked women's goods—ribbons, notions, buttons, yarn, gewgaws—as well as equipment like brooms and men's goods like razor strops. A sewing-machine agent, like earlier peddlers, would have access to women as well as men, would have reason to call at people's houses at all times of day or week, and so Ratliff could readily strike up banter or barter with any citizen of Yoknapatawpha County, male or female, black or white, of whatever rank or social standing. Further, he would be especially apt at ingratiating himself with women. He must be able to empathize, be open to a range of feeling—sympathy, kindness, concern—more typical of women than of men in a near-frontier society such as that in which he would drive his buckboard. These traits were incipient in the agent in *Father Abraham*, but Faulkner was not yet ready to develop him in these directions, no doubt because unready himself to perceive the Snopeses with such a range of feelings as Ratliff would eventually experience.

In *The Hamlet* Ratliff's broad and sympathetic sensibility in no way compromises his masculine traits or his acceptance by men.

> He spoke in a pleasant, lazy, equable voice which you did not discern at once to be even more shrewd than humorous. . . . He sold perhaps three machines a year, the rest of the time trading in land and livestock and second-hand farming tools and musical instruments or anything else which the owner did not want badly enough, retailing from house to house the news of his four counties with the ubiquity of a newspaper and carrying personal messages from mouth to mouth about weddings and funerals and the preserving of vegetables and fruit with the reliability of a postal service. He never forgot a name and knew everyone, man mule and dog, within fifty miles.   (13)

Thus Ratliff is an inveterate trader as well as news-bearer. And in these parts, trading is the universal masculine pastime and assertion of self. In matching wits against another man's, a fellow establishes his *bona fides* by the way he conducts himself in this business; Yoknapatawpha's is not a cash economy but one in which trading looms large, and the man who can hold his own in the trader's agile play of wit, who knows the relative value of every object or creature that comes to hand, who keeps his composure and comes out ahead—such a man is worthy of his neighbor's respect.

Ratliff's shrewd anecdotal manner, his purposeful meandering through byways toward an often-concealed meaning, establishes the style of *The Hamlet*. That style is not merely conversational but uses the very cadences of the tale-teller, the spinner of yarns. *The Hamlet* is one long intricate yarn told from Ratliff's buckboard, in his restaurant in Jefferson, on the gallery of Varner's store. The language is spiced with folk colloquialisms, and yet this country down-home aspect of the work is thoroughly integrated into its mode as modernist fiction.

This integration, as I have suggested, was hard won. Over the years Faulkner kept trying to work up the Snopes material, publishing two short stories closely related to the "Father Abraham" manuscript: "Fool About a Horse" (1936) and "Barn Burning" (1939). In the latter Ab Snopes deliberately walks through manure and then across his landlord Major de Spain's fine carpet; after Ab's hulking daughters ruin the carpet while cleaning it and de Spain sues him for damages, Ab torches his landlord's barn. The chief character, however, is Snopes's young son Sartoris, who is so shamed by his father's shiftlessness and treachery that he runs away from his family. As Warren Beck has shown, it is proof of Faulkner's mastery of his own material that when he came to write *The Hamlet* he rejected "Barn Burning" as its opening chapter, for to have used it would have shifted the reader's attention to young Sartoris, the only Snopes so unlike his tribe. Instead, the novel begins with Ab's arrival at Frenchman's Bend, his signing on as tenant farmer with Will Varner's son Jody, and then Ratliff's telling Jody the tale of Ab's alleged association with the burning of Major de Spain's barn.[7]

The arrival in Frenchman's Bend of such strangers as the Snopeses is a matter of great curiosity, especially since Ab's incendiary reputation has accompanied (or preceded) his migration hither. Ratliff, we learn, is the only one in the hamlet who knew Ab Snopes of old, and he tells the loungers on the veranda of Varner's store what Ab was like before he "soured," and how his disposition was turned. Here Faulkner rewrites his short story "Fool About a Horse," making Ratliff (rather than the son of the unnamed trader in the story) the narrator and participant in the action. When Ratliff was a boy of eight, Ab Snopes, then married to his first wife and childless, lived on the next tenant farm to Ratliff's father's. Ab was not then the mean-spirited, grudging sorehead who stomps across de Spain's rug or into Varner's store—he was an amiable horse trader, and it was his being bested in a hoaxing horse swap by the renowned dealer Pat Stamper that squeezed the good nature out of him, coming as it did after "that business during the War" (in *The Unvanquished*)

7. Faulkner, "Fool About a Horse," in Joseph Blotner (ed.), *Uncollected Stories of William Faulkner* (New York, 1979), 118–34; Faulkner, "Barn Burning," in *Collected Stories* (New York, 1948), 3–25; Warren Beck, *Faulkner* (Madison, Wis., 1976), 179–80. Blotner describes the composition of "Fool About a Horse" and the differences between the text as published in *Scribner's Magazine* (August, 1936) and in Part 2, Chapter 2, Book One, of *The Hamlet*, in *Uncollected Stories*, 684–85.

when "Ab had to withdraw his allegiance to the Sartorises." Ratliff recalls that Ab "at least had horse-trading left to fall back on. Then he run into Pat Stamper. And Pat eliminated him from horse-trading. And so he just went plumb curdled" (29).

The auction of the spotted ponies, the main action of the last of the novel's four sections, is an extended replication of the contest of wits at the beginning—Ab Snopes's defeat in horse trades with Pat Stamper. The Snopes-Stamper contest had been dimly prefigured in Jody Varner's clumsy attempt to outwit Flem by hiring him to help out at the store, a move Jody misconstrues as a fire insurance policy. The Snopes-Stamper trades serve as fitting prelude to Ratliff's efforts to get the better of Flem—not, as with Jody, to gain by it, but, because Ratliff is the moral center of the story, to take the measure of a man he perceives as an evil force in the community.

THE HORSE SWAP

Revising "Fool About a Horse" for inclusion in *The Hamlet*, Faulkner again showed his mastery of his novel's design. He changed things just enough to make the tale integral to *The Hamlet*; the intricate plot remains intact. It has been suggested that Augustus Baldwin Longstreet's story "The Horse Swap," from *Georgia Scenes* (1835), is the source, or a source, for Faulkner's yarn. What is likelier is that Faulkner, like Longstreet a century earlier, heard the tale, or others like it, for there was a strong and varied vein of folk anecdote concerning horses, horse swaps, and traders. Faulkner would have heard these yarns as a boy, listening to the loungers in his father's livery stable. (Murry Falkner, with his usual luck, went into the livery business just when automobiles were coming into use; this historical moment is recaptured in Faulkner's last novel, *The Reivers* [1962].) In Faulkner's tale Ab Snopes, with young Ratliff riding beside him, sets out with his wife's $24.68 to buy her a separator on which she has set her heart. Ab has hitched up his landlord's mule with a horse he got in a trade from Beasley Kemp. Learning from some gawkers at a store along the way that Beasley's horse had once belonged to Pat Stamper, that Beasley had paid $8.00 boot for it, and that Stamper is camped nearby, Ab undertakes to trade against Stamper, not to gain by it, but for the honor of the whole county. For eight dollars in cash had changed hands, and Ab sets himself "to vindicate it."

As in the contests yet to come between Flem and Ratliff, the horse trade between Ab and Stamper pits one experienced trickster against another. Ab knows the dodges of the trade—inserting a fishhook in the horse's shoulder just where dropping the reins will make the beast step lively, applying coal tar to where the horse's skin has been torn by barbed wire, rubbing his gums with ginger to make him foam like an alert animal. But against Stamper, already a legend in his own time, Ab hasn't a chance. In cahoots with his "nigger magician," a hostler who can change a horse's appearance in a trice, Stamper practices his trade. An instantaneous judge of both horseflesh and human character, Stamper knows in a moment he has got Ab in a corner when, in response to Ab's proposing a trade for his horse, Stamper offers to trade not only for Beasley's horse but for the team—that horse plus the landlord's mule. For them Stamper offers a pair of "matched" mules, neither as good as the one Ab already has but together making a tolerable-looking team.

In the event, the mules, never before harnessed together, barely make it to Wheatleaf's store, where, on being tightly tied to a post, they lie down and nearly choke. Everyone recognizes Stamper's inoperable team; Ab is the butt of much ridicule. He gives young Ratliff six bits to fetch him a bottle of whiskey. Fortified, he manages to get the mules back to Stamper's camp, for he now desperately wants to trade them back for his original team. Custom requires that the only way to undo a bad trade is to trade again. Stamper tells Ab he has already traded off both the horse and the mule, but offers Ab another mule and another horse. To make this trade Stamper requires boot—Miz Snopes's separator. The horse now offered is colored dark brown and is "hog fat," so fat it can scarcely walk.

Ab is in a box; he has to take this team. By now he is quite drunk, and it has started to rain. He passes out and young Ratliff takes the reins, turning in at the first sheltering barn. In disbelief, he sees the horse has changed color. It was brown, but it's bay-colored now. Ab wakes up, puts his hand out to touch it, and feels a spot that makes the horse plunge wildly against the wall. "I could even feel the wind in my hair. Then there was a sound like a nail jabbed into a big bicycle tire. It went *wishhhhhh* and the rest of that shiny fat black horse we got from Pat Stamper vanished . . . it was the same horse we had left home with that morning. . . . We even got our fishhook back, with the barb still bent where Ab had bent it. . . . But it wasn't until next morning that Ab found the bicycle pump valve under its hide just inside the right foreshoulder" (43).

On their arrival home with neither separator nor $24.68, "Miz Snopes began to cry." But next day she hitches up mule and horse and sets out alone. Returning in a neighbor's wagon, she gets out, pushes her cow on board, and sets out a second time. At last she comes home with her separator, for which she has traded the horse and mule plus the cow as boot. Young Ratliff brings her a pail of milk from his father's cow, and Miz Snopes runs it through her separator over and over. Ab says, "It looks like she is fixing to get a heap of pleasure and satisfaction outen it" (47). He "wasn't curdled then," but soon became so. What curdled Ab was not so much the ignominy of being bested by Pat Stamper, who after all is famous as the premier trader; what curdled Ab was the destruction of his own renown. What reputation Ab enjoyed (as we know from *The Unvanquished*) rested on his having sold back to the Union Army the same mules he had commandeered from them. And now the whole county is mocking him because Stamper has caught him with the same trick.[8]

Readers remote from the conventions of the horse swap may

8. In his anthology of horse-trading folklore collected by the Nebraska Federal Writers Project, Roger L. Welsch notes that "Almost a fourth of the stories in this corpus carry the theme of the back-trade," for, as one informant remarked, "a good trader could always count on getting back [his] horse for a song" (*Mister, You Got Yourself a Horse* [Lincoln, Nebr., 1981], 26; *vide, e.g.,* 27–37, 89–91, 101–105).

think that Faulkner has really pulled the long bow by having Stamper and his "nigger magician" paint and inflate Beasley Kemp's horse past recognition. In fact, all of the strategems used by both Ab and Stamper are traditional, documented in the extensive literature going back to the early nineteenth century which either warns the unwary against the dodges of unscrupulous horse traders or recounts the hoodwinking of a naïf by a sharp trader or, as in Longstreet's sketch, the tricking of each trader by his opponent. The conventions of horse trading, even to the master trader having a Negro accomplice adept at changing the appearance of the animals, are known in this lore, which William Ferris has surveyed in England and Ireland, and among gypsies, as well as in the South, the East, and the West in this country;[9] Roger L. Welsch has published a collection of lore from Nebraska horse traders in the early years of this century in which many of Faulkner's motifs appear. Faulkner does exaggerate the inflation of the horse (what is documented is the insertion of air in the loose skin under the shoulders);[10] but for the rest—fishhook, tar, ginger, and paint—all these dodges are traditional. In describing the psychology and language of the traders Faulkner draws closely upon traditional models too.[11]

9. William Ferris, director of the Institute for the Study of Southern Culture, University of Mississippi, kindly gave me access to his manuscript "Ray Lum: Trader." This work combines a biography of a renowned Mississippi horse and mule trader (a real-life Pat Stamper) with a comprehensive study of the printed and oral traditions of this métier. In his sketch "The Horse Trader," S. G. Thigpen describes a Negro trader whose methods further illustrate the tradition (*A Boy in Rural Mississippi* [Picayune, Miss., 1966], 166–71).

10. Evidently this was a well-known dodge. Welsch, *op. cit.*, 126–27, reprints a caution to the buyer against this trick from R. C. Barnum, *The People's Home Library* (Cleveland, 1914). Blotner, in *Faulkner: A Biography* (2 vols.; New York, 1974), I, 134, cites an advertisement in the Oxford *Eagle* (January 20, 1910) for a book entitled *Horse Secrets* by Dr. A. S. Alexander. Alexander's warning about inflation, as well as another passage describing a back-trade, is quoted by Stephen R. Portsch in "All Pumped Up: A Real Horse Trick in Faulkner's *The Hamlet*," *Studies in American Fiction*, IX (1981), 93–95.

11. Ferris has issued a long-playing recording entitled *Ray Lum: Mule Trader* with accompanying transcript of his talk and an essay about him that give a firsthand sense of the tradition and milieu (Center for Southern Folklore, Memphis, 1977).

THE GOAT TRADE

At the advent of Flem, Ratliff had said to Will Varner, "'There aint but two men I know can risk fooling with them folks. And just one of them is named Varner. . . .' 'And who's the other one?' Varner said. 'That aint been proved yet neither,' Ratliff said pleasantly" (28). In his affable way Ratliff assumes the challenge of matching wits with Flem. At first, it seems, he does so from his own love of competitive trading, but as he gets into the string of intricate deals and sees the true character of his adversary, a deeper feeling motivates him.

It all begins when Ratliff goes out of his way to sell a sewing machine to Flem's hardscrabble cousin Mink Snopes. Mink hasn't got a dime but offers as payment two promissory notes: one, for $20, is Flem's note to Mink; the other, for $10, is Isaac Snopes's note, signed with his mark, made out to him or bearer, signed Flem Snopes, and endorsed by Mink to V. K. Ratliff. These, Mink says, are to be delivered to Flem along with a message: "From one cousin that's still scratching dirt to keep alive, to another cousin that's risen from scratching dirt to owning a herd of cattle and a hay barn. To owning a herd of cattle and a hay barn" (76). Ratliff recognizes this none-too-subtle veiled threat of Mink's to burn Flem's barn—evidently Mink couldn't get Flem to pay the $20 owed him. On returning to Frenchman's Bend, Ratliff sets in motion his fiscal duel with Flem.

Ratliff has a contract from a goat rancher for 50 goats at 75¢ each, and he knows of the only herd in the county. Now, on the porch of Varner's store, in his desultory way he tells about the goat rancher lacking goats and mentions that Uncle Ben Quick has the very herd the man needs. As Ratliff foresees, Flem overhearing this rushes out to Quick's and buys the fifty goats. Now Flem owns fifty goats but has no idea who will pay to take them off his hands except Ratliff. And Ratliff offers Flem his own note to Mink for $20. Hearing the message from his cousin, Flem surrenders his bill of sale for the goats. Ratliff then burns Flem's $20 note and produces the second note for $10. Flem tells him to wait, then goes out and returns with someone else. Ratliff, looking on, feels "something black . . . a suffocation, a sickness, nausea."

He was back beside the desk now. He believed he could hear the dragging block long before he knew it was possible, though presently he did hear it as Snopes entered and turned, moving aside, the block thumping against the wooden step and the sill, the hulking figure in the bursting overalls blotting the door, still looking back over its shoulder, entering, the block thumping and scraping across the floor until it caught and lodged behind the counter leg where a three-year-old child would have stooped and lifted it clear though the idiot himself merely stood jerking fruitlessly at the string and beginning a wet whimpering moaning at once pettish and concerned and terrified and amazed until Snopes kicked the block free with his toe. [Ratliff looked upon] the Gorgon-face of that primal injustice which man was not intended to look at face to face and had been blasted empty and clean forever of any thought, the slobbering mouth in its mist of soft gold hair.   (85)

This idiot cannot even say its own name. Ike, Mink, and Flem had each received $10 when their grandmother died, and Flem, as Ike's guardian, has taken charge of Ike's note and already sold it twice. Ratliff determines not to let Flem go on using Ike's money, so he puts a match to this note too.

Flem is Ike's guardian, but the idiot is actually in the care of Mrs. Littlejohn, proprietress of the boarding hotel, where he sleeps in her barn and does simple chores. Although Ratliff is at first sickened by the very sight of Ike, he now calculates the profit he has made on his dealing with Flem and turns this money over to Mrs. Littlejohn to keep for Ike's use. She doesn't even count it, nor does he expect her to do so; decent folk trust one another. Ratliff asks her to give a message to Will Varner: "Just tell him Ratliff says it aint been proven yet neither. He'll know what it means" (87). What it means is, Ratliff knows he has bested Flem, indeed humiliated him, but he knows, too, that this is not the end of the matter.

What *has* been proven, thus far, is that Flem is heartless and Ratliff is a man of innate decency who willingly forfeits his profit for the sake of a helpless creature of whom Flem takes advantage, as he does of everyone else, idiot or not. What is also proven is that in Ratliff Flem has an opponent worthy of his mettle. The arithmetic involved in this series of deals—selling the sewing machine for the notes, buying the goat contract for Flem's $20, forfeiting the $10 note plus its three years' interest, balancing that against the sale of the goats to the rancher—all this is so complicated that Cleanth Brooks in his first book on Faulkner invoked an accountancy expert to trace the movement of moneys and values through the serial transactions.[12] Ratliff keeps all this straight in his head! Now aware of Ratliff's acumen, and of his competitiveness, Flem will be careful in future dealings with him. For the time being, though, the good-hearted peddler has gotten the goat of the soulless merchant.

It is time to raise the question of why Faulkner commences *The Hamlet* with the episodes just described, and whether the work is, in any recognizable sense, a novel at all, rather than, as has been alleged, a loose-jointed collection of four long tales. As with *The Unvanquished*, readers seeking a neat structure, a well-made novel observing the unities, regard this one as a collection of stories imperfectly joined to one another. Granting that *The Hamlet* is panoramic in scope with a large cast, its several seemingly separate but actually intertwined themes and skeins of action do in fact confer upon the whole an intricate structure that has the inevitability of a necessary form.

As every reader perceives, in *The Hamlet* there are two main themes, one an exploration of greed, the other of love. Thus far I have been concerned with the development of Ratliff and the Snopeses, the chief participants in the tales of greed. Eula Varner in her role as a comedic fertility goddess, her suitors, her marriage, and the counterpointed loves of three men—Jack Houston, Mink Snopes, and Ike—comprise the personae whose relationships embody the love theme. The ways that Faulkner has entwined these rival plots and subplots, with greed played out in an exclusively masculine milieu while love of course requires

---

12. Cleanth Brooks, *William Faulkner: The Yoknapatawpha Country* (New Haven, 1963), 402–406.

the presence of the beloveds, females, are at once subtle and bold. The combinations of these plots and themes establish the design and contribute to the range of *The Hamlet*, as the sudden shifts between one part of the saga and another help to give the work its variety of tone, keeping the reader ever off balance and intrigued.

These intertwinings are enclosed within a series of thematic brackets. The first thing we learn about the Old Frenchman's Place is Will Varner's saying "This is the only thing I ever bought in my life I couldn't sell to nobody" (6); at the end of the novel Ratliff, with Bookwright and Armstid, have bought the place from Flem Snopes because "There's something there"—buried treasure—"Will Varner knows. . . . If there wasn't he wouldn't never bought it. . . . And I knowed it for sho when Flem Snopes took it" as part of Eula's dowry (335). Ab Snopes's desecration of Major de Spain's rug leads to de Spain's going to law to get a judgment against Ab; this makes inexorable Ab's revenge—burning de Spain's barn—and in turn leads to Jody Varner's effort to insure his father's barn against combustion by hiring Flem to help mind his store. Major de Spain's experience of the futility of going to the law is twice reiterated in the penultimate chapter, when the suit of Mrs. Tull for damages caused to her husband and his wagon by the stampede of Flem's ponies is dismissed on a technicality, as is Mrs. Armstid's effort to recover from Flem her last five dollars, which her crazed husband had bid on a wild horse at the auction. Along the way we find Jack Houston's suit against Mink for the trespass of Mink's cow; although the judge decides for Houston, since the defendant was a Snopes the plaintiff gains nothing from the law. Ab had torched the major's barn; Mink murders Houston. The theme of the futility of the law as arbiter of differences striates the whole novel.

LOVE IN YOKNAPATAWPHA

Eula. Eula. Of course it was not Will Varner and his missus who gave this not-uncommon name to their infant daughter but that master of onomastics, William Faulkner, who, unlike the parents, already knew her destiny as a personification of "some symbology out of the old Dionysic times" (95), as "the supreme primal uterus" (114). Surely her euphonious name is intended to suggest the ironical echoes of Eulalie, Poe's wraithlike maiden, and of Ulalume, his all-obsessing ghost of lost love. The vibrant sexual energies that ripple through Poe's lines are there disguised and sublimated, but in Faulkner there is no such idealization or avoidance of physicality. Eula is a swamp of swollen hormones.

Eula is described simultaneously as a cartoon character and as a fertility goddess. In these divergent descriptions Faulkner seems on the one hand to be setting her down in the spirit of satirical mockery in which he and Phil Stone first conceived of his caricaturing all the rednecks, and on the other he seems to have found irresistible the temptation to mythologize, even to deify, this buxom country girl who represents the spirit of Demeter. Much later, when her father (a homeopathic veterinarian as well as a storekeeper) is on his way to set Henry Armstid's broken leg, we learn that Mrs. Varner had shown her "nekkid belly" to the full moon when carrying Eula, a ritual guaranteed to advance the fertility of all crops. The effect of both belittling Eula into caricature and bestowing upon her femaleness the aura of divinity is to distance her from ordinary human womankind. Mocked and revered almost in the same breath, she is larger than life.

It is intrinsic to Faulkner's design that this living fertility symbol not find an adequate mate among the men who are irresistibly attracted to her. Her first suitor, Labove, is an embodiment of the Protestant work ethic, driving himself to get an education and a law degree while teaching school at Frenchman's Bend. To this gaunt scholar-athlete, a football player who enjoys neither the game nor his studies, Eula "would transform the very wooden desks and benches themselves into a grove of Venus" (114). Labove is driven mad with desire for her—not love, but lust; "he wanted her one time as a man with a gangrened hand or foot thirsts after the axe-stroke which will leave

him comparatively whole again" (118). Deciding to leave the
Bend after gaining his law degree, Labove is overwhelmed by the
memory of Eula's female magnetism when his landlady in Jefferson offers him a potato, for he remembers Eula eating her daily
cold potato with all the intensity the madeleine summoned up
in Proust. So back he goes to teach school, until one day, when
Eula stays after class, he attempts to rape her. For one so inert
she proves strong as an ox, knocking the football player down
and saying "Stop pawing me, you old headless horseman Ichabod
Crane" (122)—thereby revealing she has learned *something* in
his class. Labove awaits her brother to come with pistol or gun
to avenge her honor. But Jody does not come. The next day,
when Eula returns to school as though nothing has happened,
Labove realizes she hasn't even bothered to tell; what he tried to
do was completely insignificant to her. This humiliation is too
much for Labove, who locks the schoolroom, hangs the key on a
nail beside the door, and disappears from Frenchman's Bend.[13]

Half the county is mooning over Eula, and three young men get
up the nerve to come courting. Of these, one, Hoake McCarran,
is a bully, a roustabout, a womanizer, all in all a bad lot. But he
is no coward. When he is sparking Eula in his buggy, the two
other would-be swains lie in wait and from ambush attack him
with wagon spokes and brass knuckles. McCarran gives a good
account of himself while Eula bashes his assailants with the
handle of the buggy whip. McCarran's arm is broken in the
melee, and Eula brings him home so her father can set it. After
doing so, Will, who has had his toddy, goes upstairs to bed, but
Eula and McCarran make love on the floor, she propping up his
wounded side. During this, her only experience of sexual inter-
course in the novel, Eula's child is conceived.

Once her pregnancy becomes known, however, Hoake Mc-

13. Perhaps basing his interpretation of Irving's "The Legend of Sleepy Hollow" on Chapter 4 of *Form and Fable in American Fiction*—the rivalry between
Ichabod Crane and Brom Bones for the hand of Katrina Van Tassel embodies the
traditional conflict between Yankee and frontiersman—Cecil Eby sees Labove as
Ichabod, Eula as Katrina, and Hoake McCarran as Brom Bones ("Ichabod Crane
in Yoknapatawpha," *Georgia Review,* XVI [1962], 465–69).

Carran lights out for Texas. And so do the other two suitors, as if to cast upon themselves the guilt for successful courting. None of this lot is a suitable husband for Eula Varner, though her father has to find one for her in a hurry. He has not far to look—his own clerk, Flem Snopes, is at hand and available, for a price. A deed of land, title to the Old Frenchman's Place, a cash settlement, and Flem and Eula depart by train, also for Texas.

Seeing Will Varner, Eula, and Flem in the chancery clerk's office, Ratliff didn't follow them to the circuit clerk's to witness the marriage. "He did not need to. He knew what was happening now" (147)—the transfer of property from Varner to Flem—instead he goes to the station, to see the couple depart. Had Ratliff lived in Frenchman's Bend, Faulkner writes, "he would have known no more—a little lost village, nameless, without grace, forsaken, yet which wombed once by chance and accident one blind seed of the spendthrift Olympian ejaculation and did not even know it" (147). And he beholds Eula's face: "It had not been tragic, and now was not even damned, since from behind it there looked out only another mortal natural enemy of the masculine race. And beautiful: but then, so did the highwayman's daggers and pistols make a pretty shine on him" (149). Eula, betrayed, unaware of her own potential divinity, "vanished" as the train window moves past "in retrograde . . . merely a part, a figment . . . of [her] translation" from goddess to "only another mortal natural enemy" of men. Ratliff's last impression as the honeymooners' train pulls away is "only the straw bag, the minute tie, the constant jaw" of Flem (149). Without transition Faulkner's prose becomes italicized as we move from the train platform inside Ratliff's mind—whether a daydream on the spot or a nightmare as he later contemplates the doings of that day.

Flem is in Hell, hectoring the devil for the return of his soul as per their signed contract. Here follows Faulkner's elaboration of an American folktale variant of the Faust legend, itself based upon a widespread European folktale. In the Faust legend and in its oral and literary descendants (such as Irving's "The Devil and Tom Walker"), a man makes a rash bargain with the devil, selling his soul for riches and/or power, then tries in vain to escape delivery when the due date draws nigh. The American folktale variant plays this theme to a different conclusion, as we see from this yarn taken down during the Depression by a member of the Mississippi Federal Writers Project staff from an informant in Marion County:

A prominent merchant of Columbia dreamed that he died and went to hell. The devil kindly took him on a tour of observation. He saw many strange sights, such as some of his former townsmen being boiled in oil, some dancing on a red-hot stove as big as the courthouse. At last he came to a huge iron tub with great weights piled on it.

"I'd like to see what's under the tub," he said to the devil. This gentleman evidenced much apprehension, the sweat breaking out on his brow.

"No, no," he cried, "Don't touch that! I've got Mr. Ed Lampton under that tub and if he gets out he'll have a mortgage on half of hell in less than a week."[14]

Here we have the ebullient American mercantile spirit besting the Prince of Brimstone. This reflects both the comic exaggeration of the booster spirit in American popular culture and the difference between our secular time and the faith-ridden Middle Ages. Faulkner appropriates the energies and simple plot of this folktale for Ratliff's dream, restoring to the motif the intensity dissipated in its provenience as jokelore. For Flem is aggrandized to mythic dimensions as he proves shrewder than the Prince of Darkness himself. He has come to redeem his soul, but the subdevils cannot find it—"it wasn't no big one to begin with nohow"—and the asbestos matchbox in which they sealed it is empty: "He dont want no more and no less than his legal interest according to what the banking and the civil law states in black and white is hisn. He says he has come prepared to meet his bargain and signature, and he sholy expects you of all folks to meet yourn" (149, 150). When the Prince summons Flem to tell him that he has no soul, Flem counters, "Is that my fault?" When the Prince responds, "Do you think I created you?" Flem says,

14. Typescript in RG 60, Box 121, Federal Writers Project Files, Mississippi State Department of Archives and History.

"'Then who did?' And he had the Prince there and the Prince knowed it." The devil then tries to bribe Flem, naming "all the temptations, the gratifications, the satieties," even showing Flem "his self performing them all, even the ones he hadn't even thought about inventing to his-self yet, until they was done, the last unimaginable one." But Flem "just turned his head and spit another scorch of tobacco onto the floor." Flem is beyond the reach of any temptation or sin that would entrap a *man*. The struggle between him and the Prince is being fought on his own turf, a contest of bargainers' wits. Now the Prince asks, "What do you want, Paradise?" Flem says he "hadn't figured on it. Is it yours to offer?"

"Then whose is it?" the Prince says. And the Prince knowed he had him there. In fact, the Prince knowed he had him all the time, ever since they told him how he had walked in the door with his mouth already full of law. . . . "You have admitted and even argued that I created you. Therefore your soul was mine all the time. And therefore when you offered it as security for this note, you offered that which you did not possess and so laid yourself liable to—"

"I have never disputed that," he says.

"—criminal action. So take your bag and—" the Prince says. "Eh?" the Prince says. "What did you say?"   (152–53)

And now Flem has the Prince, for Flem has proved their contract enforceable. The Prince, used to dealing with men with souls, is so discombobulated by Flem's sangfroid that "he can feel his self grabbing and hauling at his throat to get the words out like he was digging potatoes outen hard ground. 'Who are you?' he says, choking and gasping and his eyes a-popping up at him setting there with that straw suitcase on the Throne among the bright, crown-shaped flames. 'Take Paradise!' the Prince screams, 'Take it! Take it!'" and the Prince is left in the darkness of the wind, "clawing and scrabbling at that locked door, screaming" (153).

Thus, Flem, a creature born with no soul, acting entirely from his own nature, bests the devil and wins Paradise. This vision, true to Ratliff's own imagination, dramatizes his grief at the betrayal to the spirit of greed and gain of Eula Varner's potentiality as divine fertility spirit, intrinsic though that be with her natural-born antagonism to "the masculine race." The Prince of Darkness, however, although he seems not to know it, wins in the end, for Flem is impotent and cannot, ever, enjoy Eula, the Paradise he has wrested from his Adversary in Hell.

Ratliff, knowing subconsciously how soulless is Flem Snopes, should be warned thereby in his own dealings. But if Flem can outwit and hornswoggle the very Prince of Darkness, how can any man—even one as deeply moral and commonsensible as V. K. Ratliff—be proof against his wiles?

While Yoknapatawpha County is bereft of its fertility goddess and her impotent Vulcan, we meet three other pairs of lovers. Mink Snopes, whom Ratliff had compared to other Snopeses as one would a cottonmouth to other snakes, had married a strapping woman, daughter of the owner of a lumber camp where he worked; although she had given her favors to many a lumberjack before Mink, she yet proves to be a good wife to this miserable bottom dog. His fate is entwined with that of his neighbor Jack Houston, onto whose land Mink's heifer has wandered. In a sticklebacked argument over grazing rights, Houston gets a court judgment against Mink, thereby instigating Mink's revenge—a shot from ambush. But first we learn of Houston's wife, who after only three months of marriage had been killed in the barn by the stallion Houston gave her as a wedding present (an odd gift, it would appear), and how he had known her all his life, had been tutored by her in school, had run away from his fate of marrying this girl who looked after him, had lived for years with a prostitute, had on his father's death abandoned her and returned home, had (like Sutpen) thought that by dividing his savings with the abandoned woman he had made things square with her. Then after a year he had married the woman to whom he gave the stallion that kicked her to death when she entered his stall seeking one of her hens. Surely this stallion represents an intractable, untameable, male principle, an extension of

Houston's own character, for though an honorable man by his own lights, he is inflexible in his narrowly defined masculinity. This is not to say he is not moved to grief; he is in fact another of Faulkner's Mississippi Puritans, living since his wife's death in monklike asceticism.

Hyatt Waggoner has remarked on the vein of sentimentality that runs through the love stories of Mink and Houston—both involved with whores who resemble Bret Harte's faithful though fallen women.[15] Despite Houston's being so much more intelligent, solvent, and civil than Mink, he and Mink are much alike in their unbending selfhood—neither will give an inch to the other—as well as in their attraction to the same type of woman. Although Mink's wife tries to help him escape after the murder—even sleeps with Will Varner to gain the ten dollars for his train fare (money he throws away rather than accept from such a source)—and she visits him faithfully in jail, his story is no love story. For the wife is merely incidental to Mink's abiding passion—hatred, of Houston, of his cousin Flem who does not lift a finger to help him in his trouble. Jack Houston's story, on the other hand, is indeed a love story, but one in which not even love can assuage his raw fate, which he regards as an ironical joke played upon him by "the ultimate Risibility" but which the reader may see as the consequence of his own unyielding character.

These romances, such as they are, comprise the latter part of the book's third section, "The Long Summer"; they follow upon another pairing more immediately juxtaposed to Eula and her various suitors in Part II. Here the lovers are Ike Snopes, the idiot incapable of dislodging the toy he was dragging when it got wedged behind the leg of a counter, and his beloved. On a first reading of *The Hamlet* one is astonished at the elevated diction, the high romantic tone, the allusions to Hera—and at having to read almost two pages before an offhand mention of hooves reveals that the love object so defined is a cow. Faulkner recounts the courtship of an idiot stock-diddler in a style derived from

15. Hyatt Waggoner, *William Faulkner: From Jefferson to the World* (Lexington, Ky., 1959), 189–90.

blending *Jurgen* with *Idylls of the King*. His purpose in presenting such wild discrepancy between bestial infatuation and delicacy of feeling, attributing the latter to a blubbering dolt, has
generally been seen as parodic. The question of what is the point
of the parody is not so readily answered.

We have seen that Eula, when not being compared to a goddess, is described as mammalian, bovine; and here we find a cow
portrayed as either a beautiful woman ("Troy's Helen," 182, 186)
or a goddess ("Juno," 182). Imagistically, then, Eula and the cow
appear interchangeable. Implicit in the description of the cow and
of Ike's actions toward her are comparisons with the way Eula
is perceived and acted toward; we must consider these figures
of female "symbology" and the quality of the love that is offered them.

Farm boys fooling around with livestock is an old story, going
back perhaps to the doomed Cities of the Plain; in New England,
certainly to 1642, as Charles Olson's poem "There Was a Youth
Named Thomas Granger" reminds readers unsteeped in colonial
records. No doubt such doings were not unheard of in Mississippi. So it's plausible that a rural idiot's sexual urge would seek
gratification no woman would offer by taking advantage of a
nearby cow. Faulkner, taking advantage of this nearby depravity,
also takes advantage of the ways he may extend its implications.
We have seen that even Ratliff has to overcome his initial revulsion at the very sight of Ike Snopes; no one else save Mrs. Littlejohn is shown making such an effort. But to the cow Ike is not a
repulsive freak; he is like other men, only kinder, more generous, more tender. The cow, with her full udders, is indeed an ani-
mistic fertility figure. In that realm of pure possibility which
exists only in the spirit of an idiot lacking the normal human
capacity for contamination because immune from responsibility and hence from sin, Ike Snopes can be imagined, can be seen,
as courting, wooing, worshipping the cow. The purity of his passion has a surprising effect upon him. This idiot who drooled,
snuffled, could neither speak his own name nor follow a string to
which his toy was tied, by degrees becomes not only a sensient
but a thinking creature.

Quite unlike the helpless moron of our first encounter with him, Ike plans his rendezvous with the cow; he has the forethought to steal grain from another farmer's barn for their repast, "then . . . leaves the invisible basket where he can find it again at dawn" (186); "he gathers first the armful of lush grass, then the flowers . . . he lays the plucked grass before her, then out of the clumsy fumbling of the hands there emerges, already in dissolution, the abortive diadem" (184). Although unacquainted with the use of a halter, he is able properly to put one on the cow. When the meadow catches fire and the cow is trapped, Ike saves her.

The derivation of this last episode—Ike's rescue of the cow from the burning field—leads us to some deep imagistic associations that may point to the significance of this whole section with its bizarre combination of elevated romanticism and bestial content. Joseph Blotner has pointed out Faulkner's burlesque sketch "Afternoon of a Cow" (1937) as the original version of the rescue motif. In "Afternoon" the cow's samaritan is Faulkner himself, the story told by his alter ego, Ernest V. Trueblood. "Afternoon of a Cow" is itself derived, at a distance, from Faulkner's early poem "L'Après-Midi d'une Faune" (1919). Just as "Afternoon" cannot be said to succeed as burlesque, "L'Après-Midi" is by no means successful as a poem. Judith Sensibar observes, as Faulkner's faun "pursues an illusion"—

> I follow through the singing trees
> Her streaming hair and clouded face
> And lascivious dreaming knees

—"The only lascivious part of the poem is that adjective. Faulkner wrote a chaste and tame version of Mallarmé's celebrated erotic vision."[16] Faulkner's poem generates no passion because it so closely echoes early Yeats, whose Celtic Twilight style ap-

16. Blotner (ed.) *Uncollected Stories*, 702–703; "L'Après-Midi d'une Faune" is reprinted in Carvel Collins (ed.), *William Faulkner: Early Prose and Poetry* (Boston, 1962), 39–40, 124–25; Judith L. Sensibar, *The Origins of Faulkner's Art* (Austin, 1984), 70.

proximated the dreamy insubstantiality of impressionist music. But the original of these Faulkner versions of an erotic pursuit— and, presumably, conquest—remained alive in his mind: the pursuit of a love object in the shape of an animal.

When we further consider that, in *The Hamlet*, Paradise is described as sexual ecstasy, and sexual ecstasy as the devil's gift, we can see how deeply Calvinist is Faulkner's imagination— Paradise being all the more desperately longed for because forbidden. Who in *The Hamlet* attains it? Eula, once, illicitly, and the idiot Ike, at last fulfilling Faulkner's pastoral fantasy of erotic pursuit, celebration, coupling—"They lie down together" (186). The persona has changed from the nameless faun in the poem to the fictive Faulkner in Ernest Trueblood's belabored joke, to Ike Snopes: at last Faulkner has found the appropriate figure of a lover to enact his fantasy inspired by Mallarmé— hence the mixture of elevation and absurdity, ecstasy and repulsion, as a poor forked fool, scorned by the world, achieves fulfillment and experiences momentary bliss.

Because Ike's passion is pure it lifts him from his prehuman level, conferring intelligence upon a hitherto intellectually incompetent creature. His love of a brute raises him from brutishness, from animality, toward humanity, because, however repellent it appears in the village, his passion is mythopoeic. The contrast is inescapable between Ike's innocent love and the lust of Eula's suitors, the horny pedant Labove, and McCarran, the irresponsible stud. Even more pronounced is the implied comparison of Ike's pure passion with Flem's inhuman lack of love, as of any other feelings save rapacity, greed, the domination of others. As Brooks says, "the horror" of the relationship between Ike and the cow "is not gratuitous," for "it is used to set off a deeper horror and a greater perversity, that of Flem Snopes."[17] Where Eula, the cow, and even Ike are all conceived of as representing fecundity, the regenerative power of nature, that power is demeaned in the lust of Eula's suitors and perverted by Flem's

---

17. Brooks, *William Faulkner: The Yoknapatawpha Country*, 181.

sterility. Flem is divorced from nature, thus monstrous. As Labove had predicted, "[Eula's] husband . . . would be dwarf, a gnome, without glands or desire," an abhuman troll (118). In his own way Flem, too, is mythic.

Faulkner's depiction of the idiot's bestial love is at the same time perverse and moving, grotesque yet believable, at once comic and romantic, repulsive yet humanizing. The point of Faulkner's parody of the literature of medieval romance is the implication that only in so degraded, risible, and conventionally abhorrent a fashion can the emotions that lead Malory's or Tennyson's Launcelot to his Guinevere be experienced in Yoknapatawpha County. In a community whose Persephone has been sacrificed out of conventionality and greed, only an idiot can be a true lover, his love of an animal raising him momentarily above his mindless animal nature. The irony in this is worthy of Cervantes, or of Swift.

The Hamlet ultimately dramatizes the failure of Frenchman's Bend to achieve or sustain love, and the consequences of this failure to its inhabitants. The idyll, or mock idyll, of Ike and the cow is destroyed by the intrusion of avarice, for when Houston delivers the cow and Ike to Mrs. Littlejohn with orders to keep them off his property, it is Lump Snopes's charging admission to watch Ike and the cow through a slit in the fence that leads to the intervention of Ratliff, I. O., and Reverend Whitfield.[18] The minister, following the precedent of another such case, proposes that the offending cow be slaughtered and her lover be forced to eat of her flesh, to cure him of his infatuation. This, alas, is done, but poor Ike is left bereft and miserable; to console him, his cousin Eck—the only Snopes with a heart—gives him a toy cow. So Ike is once again reduced to an idiot dragging a toy.

With Eula spirited away for a seeming honeymoon and enforced confinement, the Land of Lacklove becomes a rural-Mississippi, turn-of-the-century version of the Waste Land. Where love has withered, where fecundity is exiled, the passions

18. Lump's given name is Launcelot. His sideshow exhibition of Ike and the cow introduces the love idyll (163–64), although at this point we do not know what the men and boys are looking at through the hole in the fence.

that remain are avarice, lust for power, assertion of selfhood, murderous hatred. Eula's return with her baby finds the natural world brimming with fecundity—the pear tree in bloom, the mockingbird singing, the full moon flooding the summer night— but the men who have lived all these months without the avatar of fertility and the life-force among them are eager to participate in their own entrapment by Flem's agent. When the Texas auctioneer arrives with his string of wild and untameable ponies, all the men but Ratliff give in to their irrational desires and bid up the useless horses.

THE AUCTION

At first sight the men take it for a circus, the arrival of a covered wagon at the head of a multicolored procession of "horses . . . larger than rabbits and gaudy as parrots and shackled to one another . . . with sections of barbed wire . . . they huddled, gaudy motionless and alert, wild as deer, deadly as rattlesnakes" (271). Flem has returned from his unconsummated honeymoon, bringing with him this string of wild beasts and an auctioneer named Buck Hipps. The first man to approach the horses is Jody, and a pony, "faster than a boxer," rears and strikes at his face. "Hup, you broom-tailed hay-burning sidewinders," says the stranger (272).

The stage is set for a carnival. The gathered men express widespread distrust of these creatures—have they ever been ridden? don't they belong to Flem? "'Me buy one of them things?' Eck said. 'When I can go to the river anytime and catch me a snapping turtle or a moccasin for nothing?'" (282). But Buck is undismayed; wheedling and cheerfully cursing the herd, he starts the auction despite the crowd's reluctance to bid—by giving a horse to Eck, the chief doubter, for nothing. Sure enough, Eck does bid on a second pony, and the auction is on.

Just as Buck gives away the first horse, a latecomer arrives. This is Henry Armstid, poorest of the poor dirt farmers, with his patient Griselda of a wife. And Armstid insists on bidding five dollars on one of the untameable horses. His wife tries to dissuade him—the five dollars are her earnings, weaving string into cloth and selling it to save up for shoes for their little "chaps." But Armstid bids her shut up, and smacks her in full view of the silent crowd. The Texan, sizing up the situation, returns the money to Mrs. Armstid, but Flem takes it away from her. This poor abused wife and penniless mother is a figure of tragedy in the midst of the rip-roaring cavortings of the wild horses and the eager folly of their would-be purchasers.

Their bidding and its consequences represents one of the three levels of action in this fourth part, which retains Faulkner's original title, "The Peasants." We are in the world of men here, and everyone in Frenchman's Bend save Ratliff is suckered into spending hard-earned cash on the putative ownership of horses. What makes horse ownership so hard to resist is not only the status it confers or the supposed utility of these horses on the farm. As with Houston's stallion (and with horses generally in Faulkner's work), the horse embodies masculinity—in opposition, of course, to the femaleness embodied in the cow. So these otherwise experience-hardened farmers' insistent bidding on obviously unbroken and untameable horses is an irrational impulse, not to be reined in by judgment or common sense. When the last horse has been purchased, the men enter the corral to collect their new property, and, Eck's boy having left the gate ajar, the horses stampede and run wildly through the county for days.

Counterpoised to this comedy of unchecked acquisitiveness is the imperturbability of the natural world and the presence of women whose values are dramatically contrasted to those of the men. Mrs. Armstid is one of these: she represents family, prudence, loving concern for her children. The other woman present is Mrs. Littlejohn, who throughout the day and the night comes out from her hotel to do, then hang, laundry, her wash recurring every few pages as a leitmotif poised against the covetousness of the men and the chaos they bring upon themselves, in much the way that Andromache and her women washing clothes in a stream is poised, as a reminder of the tranquillity of

domestic life, against the warlike preparations of Hector and the
Trojan warriors in *The Iliad*. All of this—Mrs. Littlejohn's washing, the bidding-up of the ponies—is going on in the midst of
heedless Nature: the "mazy moonlight" casting its spell, the
pear tree "now in full and frosty bloom . . . like . . . a drowned
woman sleeping on the uttermost floor of the windless and tide-
less sea." Into this stasis the only movement is "A bird, a shadow,
fleet and dark and swift, curved across the moonlight upward
into the pear tree and began to sing; a mockingbird" (277). In this
dreamlike beauty of the silvered night the horses burst out, one
rushing wildly into Mrs. Littlejohn's hotel, confronting the as-
tounded Ratliff in the hall; another rushes over a wooden bridge,
trampling upon Mr. and Mrs. Tull, upsetting their mules and
wagon, breaking Tull's leg. Henry Armstid's leg has already been
broken, in the first rush of the crazed calico horses.

The auction is one of Faulkner's *tours de force*, the styles in
its telling balancing against each other the lassitude and dreamy
lyricism of natural description, the folk speech of the men and
the auctioneer, and the cubist impressionism describing the
sudden bursts of animal frenzy as the horses pour across the
town and countryside. In symbiosis to these comedic effects—in
one aspect the whole story is a tall tale—is the grim naturalism
of the plight of the Armstids: Henry's crazed determination to
own a horse, his abuse of his wife, her pathetic entreaties, and,
in the end, Flem's utterly heartless pocketing of her hard-won
and desperately needed five dollars. Flem had stood by, impassive and "gravely inattentive" while she pleaded with her
husband; it must be his recognition that taking her money is too
outrageous even for the festival of fools who have bought all his
other horses that makes him give her a five-cent bag of candies
"for her chaps." This is mighty cold comfort, a one percent re-
payment—not of guilt, Flem feels no guilt—to assuage public
opinion.

The auction makes us realize (if we have not already done so)
that Flem is a driven figure. Like Melville's Confidence-Man, his
wiles and deceits far exceed any visible gain he can get by them.
His pleasure transcends mere profit; it resides in knowing he has

entrapped everyone else, his own kin included. The one man in Frenchman's Bend who escapes Flem's design in the auction, as we have seen, is Ratliff. So far, two contests between them, and Ratliff is still ahead.

But he is not unscathed. The Ratliff who provided for Ike Snopes to protect him from Flem's embezzlement of his ten dollars now declines to help Mrs. Armstid, whose need is surely greater than that of an idiot who doesn't even know to search for a lost coin. "I never made them Snopeses and I never made the folks that cant wait to bare their backside to them. I could do more, but I wont. I wont, I tell you" (321). Ratliff is no longer the equable champion of the first half of the book; he has lost patience with mankind, and something of himself has been lost in the process. We see this in his third dealing with Flem.

Henry Armstid has seen Flem digging secretively at the Old Frenchman's Place. He tells Ratliff and Bookwright, and they drive out furtively to see for themselves. Sure enough, there is Flem, methodically digging. What can he be after but the treasure everyone knows was buried there during the Civil War? After Flem leaves, the three start digging, and soon they uncover a bag of coins. They enlist an old wizard with a dowsing stick to help find the rest of the treasure, but while he is dowsing they hear someone who has observed them. They now know they must buy that land at once, before the other fellow, who must know why they are out there in the middle of the night digging and dowsing. Ratliff drives off to meet Flem. Will Varner warns him—"You got better sense than to try to sell Flem Snopes anything, and you sholy aint fool enough by God to buy anything from him, are you?"—but Ratliff merely replies "I dont know," his voice "pleasant and unchanged and impenetrable" (353). Flem won't even dicker, so Ratliff has to meet his price. "Ratliff gave a quit-claim deed to his half of the side-street lunch-room in Jefferson. Armstid gave a mortgage on his farm, including the buildings and tools and live-stock and about two miles of three-strand wire fence; Bookwright paid his third in cash" (354).

Not until the deed is signed does Ratliff stop to realize that a cloth bag of coins buried for over thirty years would have rotted. He and Bookwright examine the coins: gold dollars, dated from 1871 to the year before the present. Flem had salted the mine, the oldest trick in the book—the one greenhorn Mark Twain was stung by in *Roughing It*. Not that Flem knew Ratliff and his friends would buy the place—he just dug by night until someone, anyone, saw him, knowing he could count on human nature to deliver up a sucker. Unwittingly, Ratliff, succumbing at last to the covetousness and greed of the rest of the county, has, like everyone else in Yoknapatawpha, "bared his backside" to Flem Snopes.

Flem, brought to court by two of his victims, remains imperturbable, knowing all along that the law is an ass. The judge finds him not liable for the damages done Mrs. Tull by horses she can't prove were his and which the judge finds in fact were hers. Mrs. Armstid's plea for the return of her five dollars is similarly denied since even though Henry never took possession of his horse, he took title. Now that Flem has wiped up everyone in Frenchman's Bend he sets off for Jefferson, where he is the new half-owner of a restaurant. As his wagon passes the Old Frenchman's Place Flem sees Henry Armstid, by now quite mad, frantically digging in the worthless ground. "Snopes turned his head and spat over the wagon wheel. He jerked the reins slightly. 'Come up,' he said" (366). Ratliff's nightmare has come true: completely without qualm or human feeling, Flem has indeed been diabolical in his entrapment of the soul of every man in the community.

Now Flem takes Eula away from Frenchman's Bend to Jefferson, the milieu of the next two novels in Faulkner's trilogy. Although there are effective chapters in *The Town* and its sequel, *The Mansion* (especially the section in the latter in which Mink, released from his prison term, buys a pistol and takes revenge on Flem for abandoning him), neither book has the poise or the power of *The Hamlet*. Domesticating Eula as a wife in town having an affair, reducing Flem from the sinister figure of *The Hamlet* to a sharp arriviste trying to break into Jefferson society, taking Ratliff out of his native habitat and introducing other garrulous narrators all weakens the saga by diluting its archetypal power and its intimate connections to the folk imagination. *The Hamlet* can stand alone as a masterpiece in which only the comedy makes its tragic knowledge bearable.

IV

GO DOWN, MOSES

"WAS" AND UNCLE ADAM'S COW

There is no such thing as *was*—only *is*. If *was* existed, there would be no grief or sorrow.

—William Faulkner

Faulkner's "Was" is either his most successful comic story or one of his most objectionable. Assuming for the moment the comic view, there's no denying that the characters in this knockabout farce are by Restoration Comedy out of Li'l Abner: the woman-shy old bachelor, the huntin'-gamblin' country squire, the mincing overaged coquette; add for good measure to this seamless patchwork of stereotypes the scheming servant familiar in *Commedia del'Arte*. But the venue is Dogpatch, or somewhere like it. Faulkner himself mentioned "a certain sociological importance" in defining the backcountry setting of "Was"; he wished, he says, "to show my country as it really was in those days. The Elegance of the colonial plantation didn't exist in my country. My country was still frontier. . . . People lived from day to day, with a bluff and crude hardiness, but with a certain simplicity." Every reader responds to the contrast, in "Was," between the "certain simplicity" of this near-frontier life and the complexity of plot of which it is the setting. Is it only the country setting that makes us think, as Lewis Dabney observes, that in this tale, "Through the folklore he cherishes Faulkner reaches back to the Southern frontier, subverting the official legend of the old South"?[1]

1. Frederick L. Gwynn and Joseph L. Blotner (eds.), *Faulkner in the University* (New York, 1959), 131; Lewis Dabney, "'Was': Faulkner's Classic Comedy of the Frontier," *Southern Review*, n.s., VIII (1972), 736.

The opinion that Faulkner is using, or writing, folk humor remains for the most part a general statement, unsubstantiated by demonstration of specific allegiances to folk traditions. One reason for the paucity of documentation on this head is probably the paucity of documentation available. We know from the testimony of those who knew him, those who grew up with Faulkner in Oxford, that "there was still a strong tradition of oral storytelling in the South of Faulkner's boyhood, and traces of it survive even yet. . . . Faulkner himself knew this oral tradition well, both as listener and as narrator. . . . From my own boyhood days in Oxford, Mississippi, I can well remember the aging veterans (known locally, with affectionate indulgence, as 'The Sons of Rest'), sitting under the trees around the courthouse and swapping stories about the war. But Faulkner seems to have learned even more about it from the women at home." Calvin S. Brown considers, as folktales, both the tall tale and the family reminiscence, including "Was" in the latter.[2] But this is a grouping too loosely conceived to show that Faulkner's "Was" is indeed, as Dabney terms it, a "classic comedy of the frontier."

When we seek evidence of the folktales Faulkner knew, they prove hard to pin down. We know he heard such things, and told them, among those loiterers on the courthouse steps, as well as to children at his daughter's parties, to drinking companions, and especially to friends on the annual pilgrimage to General Stone's camp in the wilderness. One such fellow hunter reports: "Sometimes at night he'd tell stories. He'd tell some tall tales like the rest of us would around there—yarns and things. I don't remember too many of them. There were so many tales told I didn't try to keep up with them. He could tell some big ones all right. Some of them he kind of made up as he went along."[3] Nobody took down what Faulkner said on any of these hunting trips; in fact he was not recorded at all until he was a Visiting Writer at the University of Virginia, at Nagano, and at West

2. Calvin S. Brown, "Faulkner's Use of the Oral Tradition," *Georgia Review,* XXII (1968), 160–61.
3. Jerrold Brite, "A True-Blue Hunter," in James W. Webb and A. Wigfall Green (eds.), *William Faulkner of Oxford* (Baton Rouge, 1965), 186.

Point, where every word he said in classrooms and seminars was taped and transcribed. But that is not where folktales are told, so the best evidence we have of Faulkner's participation in the old tradition of Southern storytelling remains the pages of his fiction. As in "Was." Let us examine the text of "Was," and by a dissection which will not be a murder, since the tale is indestructible, we can look at its constituent parts to determine which are derived from folklore, and perhaps even discover from what folklore "Was," however circuitously, is descended.

This is but one of the problems with the tale, however. Having determined whether or not "Was" is in the American folk humor tradition, we must then consider whether it is simply a short story based on comic stereotypes, or is it, in some way, an appropriate opening chapter in a novel of tragic meaning? And then there is the manner of its telling: the three opening paragraphs present the rest of the tale as the total recall of an old man, Isaac McCaslin, remembering the total recall of his elder cousin McCaslin Edmonds, as Cass Edmonds had told the tale to him many years after the event. Is this device, which gives the story simultaneous closeness and distance, one of Faulkner's idiosyncratic affectations, or is it a functionally effective means of presenting what "was" and what "is," of controlling the point of view? If the latter, then why does "Was" have as its actual narrator a nine-year-old boy who tells none of the succeeding tales of *Go Down, Moses?* And finally, what is the meaning of "Was"? Is it, as some readers have maintained, a sentimental re-creation of old times on the plantation, or, as others have suggested, a black comedy in which the toying with slavery, the avoidance of adult responsibility, and the demeaning treatment of women convey the real meaning of the tale, grotesquely embedded in a seeming farandole of frontier folk humor? To answer these queries will require a definition of the kind of book *Go Down, Moses* is, whether a short story collection, a novel, or something else.

A student at Virginia, during one of those sessions in which every word was taped, asked Faulkner if he remembered the germ of his story "Was." The author replied: "The germ of the story was one of the three oldest ideas that man can write about, which is love, sex. And to me it was comic, of the man that had got himself involved in an engagement, and he himself couldn't extricate himself and . . . he had to call on his brother, and his brother used the only tools he had, which was his ability to play poker. Which to me was funny, was comic."[4] So "Was" is a love story, a comic love story. In fact it is also the story of a hunt, a quest, and a wager. Let me capitalize these, for they are the archetypal shapes that gird the structure of Faulkner's comic fable: The Hunt, The Courtships (these subsume The Quest), and The Wager that provides a solution for the predicament of "the man that had got himself involved in an engagement, and he . . . couldn't extricate himself."

The tale begins with Uncle Buck and Uncle Buddy McCaslin chasing a fox through their house; when caught it will be kept in a cage until released on a day when they feel like hunting it. But now Uncle Buck, with nine-year-old Cass, must set out on a longer hunt, for his Negro, Tomey's Turl, has run off to visit his girlfriend Tennie, who is a slave on the Beauchamp place miles away. Why does Buck go after Turl, since Mr. Hubert Beauchamp would surely return him? Because Hubert would bring with him his maiden sister Sophonsiba and would stay for a week's visit while Sophonsiba tries to entrap Buck in matrimony. In the event, that is what happens at Beauchamp's, for Tomey's Turl, in collusion with Sophonsiba, eludes capture, so Buck and Cass must spend the night, and Sophonsiba awaits Buck in the very bed he is likeliest to enter when he climbs the dark stairs. In the meantime, Buck and Hubert had made a bet, which Hubert, on a technicality, has lost. So when Hubert presses his claim that to redeem the Beauchamp honor Buck must marry the woman whose bed he had violated, the two obligations offset one another. And Buck used "the only tools he had, which was his ability to play poker." His freedom is wagered against the five-hundred-dollar bet. Or, we might say, Sophonsiba is wagered against the five hundred dollars.

4. Gwynn and Blotner (eds.), *Faulkner in the University*, 130–31.

This bare skeleton of the tale puts one in mind of an old story:

One time there was two old men that lived up Magnetic Holler, right close to a little branch they call Mystic Spring nowadays. One of these fellows was Uncle Adam, and he had a wife. The other one was knowed as Uncle Dick, and he didn't have no wife, but he had two cows. They got to trading jackknives and shotguns, and finally Uncle Adam swapped his wife for one of Uncle Dick's cows. Folks used to trade wives pretty free in them days, and nobody said much about it. Lots of them wasn't really married anyhow, so there wasn't no great harm done.

But it wasn't long till word got around that Uncle Adam's woman had up and left him, and moved all her stuff over to Uncle Dick's cabin. The next time Uncle Adam come into town, somebody asked him if Uncle Dick had stole his wife. "Hell no," says Uncle Adam, "it was a fair swap, all open and above board. Dick gave me his best cow for the old woman, and two dollars boot."

Folks got to laughing about it, and one day the sheriff stopped Uncle Adam on the street. "This here trading wives is against the law nowadays," says he. "And everybody knows a woman is worth more than a cow, anyhow." Uncle Adam laughed right in the sheriff's face. "Don't you believe it, Sheriff," he says, "don't you believe it. Why, that cow of mine is three-fourths Jersey!"

That's folklore, the way it's told by Vance Randolph, the collector of folktales from the Ozarks.[5] I could find no text closer to the Oxford courthouse steps than this, from over the state line in Arkansas. Randolph tells the tale as it was told to him by a neighbor in Eureka Springs back in 1950. The story is supposed to have really happened there about 1880, but by then the yarn was already frayed from many tellings. Annotations by the folklore scholar Herbert Halpert show that it was in print in 1800; far from being uniquely "true" in Eureka Springs, this is a tale widespread in American folklore. Faulkner wrote "Was" in 1940, twelve years before Randolph published the yarn in *Who Blowed Up the Church House?* so we can't say that the Arkansas story is the source of "Was." But it seems likely Faulkner heard it, or something similar, told as true, years before, in the environs of Oxford, Mississippi. A great writer is not so poor in invention

5. Vance Randolph, *Who Blowed Up the Church House? and Other Ozark Folktales* (New York, 1952), 42–43.

that he cannot make up the plot of a joke, if need be; should he instead prefer to use a hand-me-down from the circle on the courthouse steps, there must be reasons for his doing so, and differences between what he heard told to him and what he tells to us. Faulkner has indeed transformed what he borrowed.

Before considering his transformations, however, let it be said that Vance Randolph is a skilled folk raconteur. Reviewing his books, I pointed out long ago that he is an adept in the art—of which Mark Twain was our principal master—of seeming to speak in the vernacular.[6] Randolph lived in a community of backcountry Homers, like Lafayette County, Mississippi, and his art is an emulation of, or perhaps improvement upon, theirs. In pacing, detail, order of events, and sentence length, Randolph is almost always right. He tells the tale as it should be told: "One time there was two old men that lived up Magnetic Holler, right close to a little branch they call Mystic Spring nowadays." Already he has told us who, where, and when, the when being a good deal earlier than "nowadays." The aura of place names is introduced, and the phrase "lived . . . right close to a little branch" surely suggests that these two men lived on a mountain, far from town: up because close to Mystic Spring; far from town because the stream was still just a little branch.

Faulkner, too, has modelled his language, his syntax, the rhythms of his sentences, on the speech of country people. His purposes are more complex than Randolph's, yet his style has no more elegancies of expression than the plantations in his story have columns or porticos. His tone is that of Southern vernacular speech. But let us see what he makes of the plot he shares with Randolph's joke. Repeating the tale as it was told to him by a fellow who told it as it was told to him, Randolph makes nothing of it. He tells it for its own sake, and that's that. We may remember that Yeats, in *The Celtic Twilight*, defined folktales as "stories that have no moral."

Therefore it doesn't bother the teller that his tale is really

6. Reviews of Randolph, *We Always Lie to Strangers: Tall Tales from the Ozarks* and *Who Blowed Up the Church House?*, in *Midwest Folklore*, II (1952), 191–94, and III (1953), 251–54.

rather cruel, and crude, and sexist, and otherwise filled with socially undesirable opinions. In fact his attention may well not be
fixed on the uncompliment the story pays to Uncle Adam's wife,
and by extension to anyone else's wife or to any other woman
within hearing. But of course who would tell a joke like this
with a woman within hearing? The teller's attention is probably
fixed on Uncle Dick and Uncle Adam, on their masculine devotion to swapping, to see who gets the better end of the swap, and
on their not unattractive attitude to the law which enables
Uncle Adam to tell off the sheriff with a jest.

Nonetheless, no hearer can escape making the equation that
is the point of the story: Wife = Cow. This is of course a judgment of value. Surely the weight of the equation is repellent to
our moral sensibilities: a woman is equated to a beast, whether
of burden, of the dairy, or of pleasure. There is in the Ozark tale
the suggested connection of sex with bestiality, though to be
sure this remains veiled, implicit. The equation appears as a per-
fectly natural, taken-for-granted aspect, indeed, an expression,
of the male ethos that is the basis of the story.

In the folktale, plot is all; the characters are abstractions, mere
types. They exist for the sake of the action, and our interest is in
what happens. For Faulkner, however, character is all, and plot is
a means of revealing it. Our interest is in what happens to whom,
and why does he do what he does. Still, Faulkner's opening sentence, true to the formula of oral telling, like Randolph's sets the
scene, the place, and names the characters: "When he and Uncle
Buck ran back to the house from discovering that Tomey's Turl
had run again, they heard Uncle Buddy cursing and bellowing in
the kitchen, then the fox and the dogs came out of the kitchen
and crossed the hall into the dogs' room."[7] That's not a sentence
yet—it goes on for half a page—but it's enough to start with.
One's first question well might be, what in the Hell is happening? A pack of dogs chasing a fox from the kitchen into the dogs'
own room? And who are "he" and "Uncle Buck" and "Uncle
Buddy" and "Tomey's Turl"?

7. Faulkner, *Go Down, Moses* (1940; rpr. New York, 1983), 4. Page references
to this edition will be shown in parentheses in the text.

If we have read *The Unvanquished,* we know about Uncle
Buck and Uncle Buddy, and since Isaac McCaslin is retelling
Cass Edmonds' remembrance of what happened, "he" in this
story must be Cass. But what about "Tomey's Turl"? What a
strange way to name a child, and to keep calling him that as he
grows into manhood. But of course Tomey's Turl, in 1859, is a
slave. So it's all right to call him by an eponym otherwise appropriate to a racehorse. Or, to be more accurate, it never occurs to
anyone in the story *not* to call him that way. Probably doesn't
occur to him either. That's just the way it is. But Faulkner doesn't
merely accept everything that his tale accepts, or his characters
accept. Not that he ever says he doesn't, but if we are attentive
to the incidental detail we can sense what Faulkner's attitude is,
because he evokes an attitude in us.

This is often done by juxtaposition, as in "Tomey's Turl had
run again . . . then the fox and the dogs came out of the kitchen,"
subliminally establishing a relationship between the running of
Tomey's Turl and of the fox. And indeed, later, when Uncle Buck
and Cass have pursued Tomey's Turl to the Hubert Beauchamp
plantation, several hours' ride away, and still not found him, Mr.
Hubert unleashes his pack of hounds to track down Turl, who,
like a fox, leads the hounds a merry chase. By nightfall, "They
found that Tomey's Turl had doubled and was making a long
swing back toward the house. 'I godfrey, we've got him,' Uncle
Buck said. 'He's going to earth. We'll cut back to the house and
head him before he can den'" (17–18).

As Lewis Dabney has observed of this hunt-and-chase,
"There are rules: it is a ritual dance, appropriate to the introduction of the old regime; not, however, the predictable and de-
corous minuet, or even a gavotte, but a *courante,* a run." This
ritual dance Dabney shows to be a comic inversion of a much-
collected Negro folk narrative, which tells of the pursuit of
runaway slaves by "paterollers" whose runs were in earnest,
not in fun.[8]

It is typical of Faulkner to reverse, turn inside out, or stand on

8. Dabney, "'Was': Faulkner's Classic Comedy of the Frontier," 739.

their heads whichever conventions he borrows or steals. The whole tale is a reversal of our expectations about plantation life, so rough and ready do we find it. And Faulkner has turned inside out for his own purposes yet another strain of Negro folklore. In Joel Chandler Harris' familiar retellings, Brer Rabbit cleverly escapes from Brer Fox. But Faulkner makes Brer Fox not the pursuer but the pursued, and Tomey's Turl's knowledge of Uncle Buck, of dogs, of his mule, and of the countryside makes possible his foxlike evasion of the white squires and their pack of hounds and their fyce.

The grotesqueries of the fox-hunting imagery serve a further purpose in "Was," for the way foxes were then hunted in backcountry Mississippi was a parody of the formal English model, which Faulkner himself so enjoyed, scarlet jacket and all, both in Oxford and in the fox-hunting country of Virginia. In "Was" the fox-hunting vocabulary establishes an executive metaphor for the story, and by the inevitably satirical comparison to hunts which this one parodies, lays the groundwork for the social pretensions of Sophonsiba Beauchamp. Further, the hunting of Tomey's Turl brings into *Go Down, Moses* the theme of the hunt itself; what is here parodic and comic will become sacramental in "The Old People" and epical in "The Bear."

If hunting the runaway slave is a game, Uncles Buck and Buddy, superannuated boys, turn all of life into games. In "Was" they are comic characters, without a hint of Buck's wartime bloody-mindedness in *The Unvanquished*, which, though written earlier, takes place a few years later. Even the McCaslin twin's manumission of their slaves is a game, a ritual; these bachelor antebellum abolitionists have moved out of their father's mansion, letting free those slaves who would leave, letting live in the unfinished house the rest, whom they lock up each evening in full knowledge that the Negroes are escaping out the back way. It is a point of honor on both sides that the escapes be made not in the brothers' sight, so as not to embarrass them. Tomey's Turl has overstepped the rules by taking off for the Beauchamp place, so, according to those rules, he is pursued. It's all part of the game.

As Uncle Buck and Cass approach the Beauchamps':

They could already hear Mr. Hubert's dinner horn a mile away. . . . The boy was still sitting on the gatepost, blowing the horn—there was no gate there; just two posts and a nigger boy about his size sitting on one of them, blowing a fox-horn; this was what Miss Sophonsiba was still reminding people was named Warwick even when they had already known for a long time that's what she aimed to have it called, until when they wouldn't call it Warwick she wouldn't even seem to know what they were talking about and it would sound as if she and Mr. Hubert owned two separate plantations covering the same area of ground, one on top of the other.   (9)

This is our first intimation of Sophonsiba, who in backwoods Mississippi, inhabiting a bare farmhouse, clings to the romantic fiction that her brother, if he got his deserts, is the Earl of Warwick. This is by no means the only romantic fiction to which she clings, but let's not omit to notice that the presumed Earl is discovered dipping his bare feet in the springhouse, drinking a toddy. There is in Faulkner's story a clash between two conceptions of reality: Sophonsiba's genteel feminine version of reality as romance versus the male version of her romance as reality. Hubert, Uncle Buck, Uncle Buddy—these are the males in the story, and their world is one of the hunt, the chase, and, as we soon see, the gaming table.

One can't but feel for Sophonsiba, placed by fate in so unpropitious a place for the nurture of her fantasies of romance. She's getting on a bit, has a roan tooth, is still unmarried, and would seem to have no real prospects. But she has pluck. She has the rallying coquetry of the true Southern belle who never passes up an opportunity to be charming to a man in the hope, however insubstantial, that he may, somehow, succumb to her charms. Entering the hall in a jangle of earrings and a cloud of perfume, she greets Uncle Buck with "Welcome to Warwick."

"I just come to get my nigger," Uncle Buck said. "Then we got to get on back home."

Then Miss Sophonsiba said something about a bumble bee, but he couldn't remember that. It was too fast and there was too much of it, the earrings and beads clashing and jingling like little trace chains on a

toy mule trotting and the perfume stronger too . . . something about
Uncle Buck was a bee sipping from flower to flower and not staying long
anywhere and all that stored sweetness to be wasted on Uncle Buddy's
desert air . . . or maybe the honey was being stored up against the advent of a queen and who was the lucky queen and when? "Ma'am?"
Uncle Buck said. Then Mr. Hubert said:
  "Hah. A buck bee. I reckon that nigger's going to think he's a buck
hornet, once he lays hands on him. But I reckon what Buck's thinking
about sipping right now is some meat gravy and biscuit and a cup of
coffee. And so am I." (11)

What is notable here is that Sophonsiba's sexuality has indeed
reached a male observer—nine-year-old Cass, who is made dizzy
by her perfume and the jingling of her earrings. But as for Uncle
Buck, he takes no notice of her at all. "Miss Sophonsiba said
Uncle Buck was just a confirmed roving bachelor from the cradle
born and this time Uncle Buck even quit chewing and looked
and said, Yes ma'am, he sure was, and born too late at it ever to
change now" (11–12). Sophonsiba will not be discouraged, as
she continues her efforts at raillery with no visible success. In
this company of fox-hunters and slave-hunters she too is a
hunter—as Hubert says, a Buck-hunter.
  The hunting of Tomey's Turl is a complicated, nightlong rigmarole. Especially since he has been in the kitchen during most
of the foregoing. And when Buck and Hubert go upstairs to take
a nap before resuming the chase, little Cass finds Tomey's Turl
in the back yard. Cass warns Turl, "They're going to put the dogs
on you when they get up," but that doesn't faze him. "I got protection now. All I needs to do is to keep Old Buck from ketching
me unto I gets the word" (13).

  "What word?" he said. . . . "Is Mr. Hubert going to buy you from
Uncle Buck?"
  "Huh," Tomey's Turl said again. "I got more protection than whut
Mr. Hubert got even. . . . I gonter tell you something to remember: anytime you wants to git something done, from hoeing out a crop to getting
married, just get the womenfolks to working at it. Then all you needs to
do is set down and wait. You member that." (13)

  With this sibylline prophecy Tomey's Turl disappears, to be

pursued later in the afternoon. Cass, of course, doesn't understand Tomey's Turl's advice, and neither do we, unless, after
having finished the tale, we happen to remember it. Resuming
the hunt, Uncle Buck and Mr. Hubert have their troubles finding
Tomey's Turl. After thrashing around on various blind leads, Mr.
Hubert expostulates, "I'll bet you five hundred dollars that all
you got to do to catch that nigger is to walk up to Tennie's cabin
after dark and call him" (15). Before the words are out of his
mouth, Uncle Buck has taken him up on it: "Done!"

Tracked at last to Tennie's cabin near the house, Tomey's Turl
bursts out of it, knocking the wind out of Uncle Buck, and gets
away once more. By now Mr. Hubert is asleep, snoring, upstairs
in Warwick. The house is pitch dark when Uncle Buck and Cass
return to it. They grope their way to the stairs: "'Likely hers will
be at the back,' Uncle Buck said. 'Where she can holler down to
the kitchen without having to get up. Besides, an unmarried lady
will sholy have her door locked with strangers in the house'"
(20). Coming to a door in the darkness, Uncle Buck tries the
knob, and it turns. They can barely make out a bedstead with a
mosquito bar. Uncle Buck unbuttons his trousers and slips them
off. He "lifted the mosquito-bar and raised his feet and rolled
into the bed. That was when Miss Sophonsiba sat up on the
other side of Uncle Buck and gave the first scream" (20–21).

Hubert comes in with his candle and says to Buck: "Well,
'Filus. . . . She's got you at last." How quickly do fortunes turn
in the hunts within these hunts! Buck, a moment ago the fox
hunter of Tomey's Turl, has suddenly become the fox trapped by
Sophonsiba. As Hubert puts it: "You come into bear-country of
your own free will and accord. . . . You had to crawl into the den
and lay down by the bear. . . . After all, I'd like a little peace and
quiet and freedom myself, now I got a chance for it. Yes sir. She's
got you, 'Filus, and you know it. You run a hard race and you run
a good one, but you skun the hen-house one time too many"
(23). But just at the moment when it looks as though Uncle Buck
has been outfoxed by the heiress of Warwick and her brother,
who is as eager for a bachelorhood unencumbered by his sister's
presence as is Uncle Buck himself, just then Uncle Buck turns

foxy yet again. He recalls to Hubert their bet, made earlier in the evening, five hundred dollars against Uncle Buck's catching Tomey's Turl in Tennie's cabin. True, that's where Turl was *found*, but he wasn't *caught*. "So you aim to hold me to that fool bet," Mr. Hubert says. Uncle Buck replies, "You took your chance too" (23).

Chance is what it will hinge on, for Hubert fetches a deck of cards.

"One hand," he said. "Draw. You shuffle, I cut, this boy deals. Five hundred dollars against Sibbey. And we'll settle this nigger business once and for all too. If you win, you buy Tennie; if I win, I buy that boy of yours. The price will be the same for each one: three hundred dollars."

"Win?" Uncle Buck said. "The one that wins buys the niggers?"

"Wins Sibbey, damn it!" Mr. Hubert said. "Wins Sibbey! What the hell else are we setting up till midnight arguing about? The lowest hand wins Sibbey and buys the niggers." (24)

Uncle Buck seems a bit confused, but what about Mr. Hubert? Isn't he putting a dollar value on his own sister, the same as he has done for Tennie and Tomey's Turl? It's five hundred dollars instead of three, but what an undercutting of Sophonsiba's pretensions, to be laid out on the table, as it were, alongside the "niggers." Here is the first phase of Faulkner's appropriation of the folktale plot told in "Uncle Adam and His Cow." But whereas in Vance Randolph's story each of the men involved believed that what he would get by swapping was more desirable than what he would give, in the wager of exchange the poker game will settle, Faulkner has reversed the bettors' desires. Now each one wants to *lose* the woman, for these bettors are both bachelors from the cradle born, nor will they ever swap for a wife.

Without changing his impassive comic tone an iota, Faulkner has shown up the chauvinism of the Code of the Southern Gentleman. For it is the gentleman's code that is the basis of this action: a gentleman's word is his bond; hence Hubert is bound to honor his silly bet. And Uncle Buck is bound to marry Sophonsiba, unless, by a gentleman's agreement such as the game of poker, he should manage to win his freedom by losing the game.

But it is Hubert who loses the game, winning freedom from

living with his sister. The last card, however, is yet to be played. Uncle Buddy, Buck's brother, with whom he lives in perfect bachelorhood, is not one to let Hubert outmaneuver him just because his brother was outfoxed. Foreseeing some such crisis, he had instructed Cass to return home in case of trouble. Now, while Uncle Buck hides out in the woods as Tomey's Turl had done earlier, Cass and Buddy ride to Warwick, where Buddy will intervene with Hubert. "The only tools he had," as Faulkner said, "was his ability to play poker." We know, from *The Unvanquished*, that Buddy is a master at cards, better than Buck, for Buddy had won the game between them to determine which one should serve a hitch in the war. This time, the stakes are these: "Buck McCaslin against the land and niggers you have heard me promise as Sophonsiba's dowry on the day she marries. If I beat you, 'Filus marries Sibbey without any dowry. If you beat me, you get 'Filus. But I still get the three hundred dollars 'Filus owes me for Tennie. Is that correct?" This reverses the stakes in the first game between Hubert and Buck, in which the winner won Sophonsiba. So Hubert tells Cass to "Go to the back door and holler. Bring the first creature that answers, animal, mule or human, that can deal ten cards" (27). Only Cass doesn't need to holler, for Tomey's Turl is squatting outside the door.

What follows is the second great portrayal in "Was" of playing stud poker, the tension mounting as the cards, shuffled by Buddy, are dealt by Turl, the first card face down, the four successive cards face up. By the dealing of the fifth card we know that Hubert has received a king, two threes, an ace, and another three; Buddy, six, two, four, and five. Uncle Buddy takes a look at his face-down card, then proposes new stakes: "I'll bet you them two niggers. . . . Against the three hundred dollars Theophilus owes you for Tennie and the three hundred you and Theophilus agreed on for Tomey's Turl" (28). Hubert, not unnaturally, restates the new stakes for clarification: "If I win, you take Sibbey without dowry and the two niggers, and I don't owe 'Filus anything. If you win—" and Buddy interjects, "Theophilus is free. And you owe him the three hundred dollars for Tomey's Turl" (28).

We know how Faulkner relished these dizzying complications, the labyrinthine deals that match one set of values, one character's wits, against another's, as witness Ratliff's purchase of Ike Snopes's promissory note from Flem, and his scheme to buy a herd of goats, in *The Hamlet*. Here, in the shifting stakes of the two games of one-hand stud, there may well be Faulkner's fictional replication of the intricate negotiations he himself was involved in at the time he wrote the first draft of "Was." Harold Guinzburg of Viking Press was negotiating to lure Faulkner away from his regular publisher, Random House; Bennett Cerf, of Random, made a counter-proposal: "If Guinzburg was willing only to match the offer of a $5,000 advance on the novel and book of stories, he should withdraw. If Random House was expected to cancel the contract for the next novel, the new publisher would be expected to buy the plates for *The Hamlet* at a reasonable price and the existing stock of copies; together these would come to just over $2,900."[9] This is but one in a long series of contractual snarls with publishers, agents, and movie studios in which Faulkner was continually entangled; in life he seldom showed the acumen in getting out of such tight corners as he delighted in bestowing upon Ratliff or Amodeus McCaslin.

If Uncle Buddy has the reputation of being unbeatable at cards, Hubert is no slouch either; at the least, he is not one to plunge forward without having carefully considered consequences. Listening to Buddy's restatement of the new stakes, Hubert says: "That's just if I call you. If I don't call you, 'Filus won't owe me nothing and I won't owe 'Filus nothing, unless I take that nigger which I have been trying to explain to you and him both for years that I won't have on my place. . . . So what it comes down to is, I either got to give a nigger away, or risk buying one that you done already admitted you can't keep at home" (28). His sister's fate doesn't even enter into this calculation of his chances.

9. Joseph Blotner, *Faulkner: A Biography* (2 vols.; New York, 1974), II, 1051. The letter stating these terms reached Oxford after Faulkner had arrived in New York to negotiate in person, where surely Bennett Cerf put these proposals before him.

Then, after a long silence, he turns up his face-down card: another three.

"H'm," he said. "And you need a trey and there ain't but four of them and I already got three. And you just shuffled. And I cut afterward. And if I call you, I will have to buy that nigger. Who dealt these cards, Amodeus?" Only he didn't wait to be answered. He reached out and tilted the lamp-shade, the light moving up Tomey Turl's arms that were supposed to be black but were not quite white. . . . "I pass, Amodeus."

(29)

And the comedy ends, as all comedies should, with a marriage in prospect as, returning homeward, Cass "and Uncle Buddy and Tennie all three rode in the wagon, while Tomey's Turl led the pony" (29). The result of the many chases is that Uncle Buck has, momentarily, escaped Sophonsiba's designs, he and Uncle Buddy have reclaimed Tomey's Turl, and Tomey's Turl returns with Tennie; it was Turl's desire for Tennie that had set the entire circus in motion.

This has been rather a complicated story, what Faulkner makes of the old folktale formula. He has surrounded the bare motif with a created society; he has imbedded the trade-offs in a fully realized sense of a whole way of life. There are, however, a few points at which even the most attentive reader must suspend his disbelief. We will no doubt readily accept that Tomey's Turl has conspired with Sophonsiba to delay Uncle Buck until after nightfall so that he will have to spend the night at Warwick. We are further compelled to believe, or not to disbelieve, that Tomey's Turl is a step or two ahead of both Uncle Buddy and Mr. Hubert in anticipating the stakes and fixing the hands of cards he dealt them in their game of stud. The stakes were complicated enough for the gamblers to have to keep redefining them; to anticipate what Hubert would do if he called and won requires a really intuitive knowledge of gamesman's psychology.

Perhaps Uncle Buddy's prowess at the table is hereditary—is it possible that old Carothers McCaslin, his father and founder of the McCaslin estate and line, passed along this kind of hunch playing among his other bequests of honor and ruthlessness? If so, we may better understand why Tomey's Turl can outfigure the two cardplayers, for he has more of Carothers McCaslin's blood in his veins than does either Uncle Buck or Uncle Buddy. No wonder he has "arms that were supposed to be black but were not quite white"; no wonder Hubert had said "he wouldn't have that damn half-white McCaslin on his place even as a free gift." (Hubert is the only one who calls Tomey's Turl a McCaslin.) There is nothing in "Was" to indicate why Turl is a "half-white McCaslin," but when, in "The Bear," we, with Isaac McCaslin, pore over the half-illiterate ledgers kept by his father Buck and his uncle, Buddy, long before Isaac's birth, we learn of *"Turl Son of Thucydus @ Eunice Tomy born Jun. 1833 yr stars fell Fathers will."* This statement exemplifies Faulkner's technique of withholding information while giving it, so that the very texture of his tale is a continuing cipher to be decoded as the reader becomes aware later of clues not clear or not available when he met the puzzle in the text. The ledgers tell of the mysterious suicide of Eunice, who drowned herself on Christmas Day, 1832. We learn also that *"Tomasina called Tomy Daughter of Thucydus @ Eunice Born 1810 dide in Child bed June 1833. Yr stars fell"* (269). And *"Fathers will,"* mentioned along with Turl's birth, bequeaths a thousand dollars to this light-skinned Negro described as the son of two slaves. Isaac laboriously works his way toward the revelation half hidden in the ledgers: Carothers McCaslin had committed incest with his own half-black daughter, and so was both Turl's father and his grandfather. When Eunice realized that Carothers McCaslin, "her first lover," had made their daughter Tomasina pregnant, she drowned herself. Tomey's Turl, the clever fox, the amiable fugitive in the game of hunt-and-chase, who, on exiting from Tennie's cabin, catches his half-brother Buck as he runs into him so that Buck won't be hurt in a fall, is the fruit of Carothers McCaslin's original sin. Behind the farce and horseplay, behind the folk comedy in the bachelors' paradise of "Was," is the shadow of this double sin, for McCaslin's incestuous miscegenation was a consequence of his owning human beings as though they were livestock and treating them not as persons but as the convenient instruments of his vice.

In the comic action of "Was," there is, at a distance, a faint replication of this original offense, since the gaming squires, too, casually deal in human beings; but the vice they would use Turl and Tennie as stakes to indulge is just the opposite of Carothers McCaslin's lust. For Hubert and Uncle Buddy are each determined to avoid women, not seduce them. Theirs is the dream of perpetual boyhood in which a man never need assume the responsibilities of maturity, a way of life in which women and their dreams and demands are totally irrelevant to the men's work of the world. And that work isn't real work—they have slaves to do that—their occupation is play: either gaming or the hunt. So deep is their fear of women that Sophonsiba, too, is treated as a token, a stake, in the card game on which each wagers his freedom from having to live in her presence. Although, thanks to Buddy's intervention and to Tomey's Turl's quick hand at dealing the cards, Buck gets off free this time, in the end he succumbs, as Faulkner explained to a student at the University of Virginia: "Uncle Buck finally just gave up. That was his fate and he might as well quit struggling." [10] He accepts his fate, and becomes Isaac McCaslin's father. Tomey's Turl—as we learn in the second story in *Go Down, Moses*, "The Fire and the Hearth"—in time becomes the father of Lucas Beauchamp, the old man who in the pride of his McCaslin blood has faced down Zack Edmonds (the son of Cass, who narrated "Was") when Zack tried to take Lucas' wife.

These interconnections among the characters, their forebears and their descendants, indicate not only how intricate is genealogy down on the McCaslin plantation but how complex are the interwoven experiences among the members of both races of the family. Although *Go Down, Moses* is certainly episodic, spanning several generations, its actions ranging over eighty years, I join those who maintain that this work is a unified novel, however syncretic its structure. "Was" is designed as prologue, "Go Down, Moses" as epilogue, to the main body of the work. As Faulkner explained the book at Virginia:

It covered a great deal of time. The central character . . . was a man named Isaac McCaslin who was old at the time of the book. But this background which produced Isaac McCaslin had to be told by somebody, and so this is Ike's uncle, this Cass here is not old Ike, this is Ike's uncle. And "Was" simply because Ike is saying to the reader, I'm not telling this, this was my uncle, my great-uncle that told it. That's the only reason for "Was"—that this was the old time. But it's part of him too.[11]

As sometimes happened when Faulkner was speaking impromptu, he got a detail or two mixed up—Cass is actually Ike's elder cousin, not his uncle. Faulkner's point is that the portrait of Isaac, his principal character, required the depiction of the world into which he had been born; hence we have Cass's reminiscence, told to Ike, of the way it was.

But Faulkner has told us, "There is no such thing as *was*— only *is*. If *was* existed, there would be no grief or sorrow."[12] Therefore, Faulkner can give us the seemingly prelapsarian world into which Isaac will be born, as seen by a nine-year-old boy. The use of this juvenile point of view keeps all of the dark underside of the way it was from coming into consciousness while the unknowing, deadpan telling of the naïf narrator produces much of the comedy. Evidently the tale of the hunt and the poker games first presented itself to Faulkner in this mode, even before he had conceived of Isaac McCaslin as its auditor-redactor, hence of the need for the psychic distancing from the action that Isaac's later experiences would make necessary in *Go Down, Moses*. The first version of "Was," entitled "Almost," differs from the first chapter of *Go Down, Moses* not in plot but in the identity of some characters. Faulkner had the young narrator as Bayard

11. *Ibid.*, 38.
12. Faulkner, interview with Jean Stein vanden Heuvel, in James B. Meriwether and Michael Millgate (eds.), *Lion in the Garden* (New York, 1968), 255.

Sartoris, who, with uncles Buck and Buddy, makes that version seem a continuation of, or rather a prelude to, *The Unvanquished*, written earlier.

What Faulkner started from was a plot of folk comedy, seen through the eyes of a youthful naïf, which would at once summon nostalgia for the life of boys (however superannuated) on a frontier plantation in antebellum Mississippi and would introduce a family saga filled with the revelation of sin and its consequences. Since the tale was a courtship story as well as a hunting yarn, it led immitigably to the further—and prior—history of a family. But which family? By the time Faulkner had written "Delta Autumn," which appears as the sixth, penultimate chapter in *Go Down, Moses* (the tales were not written in their order in the book), he had made Isaac McCaslin a principal character. Now Isaac seized Faulkner's imagination, as he rewrote another story, "The Old People," in which Isaac replaces Quentin Compson as the youth initiated into the hunt by shooting his first deer.[13] And it is not the Compson or the Sartoris family but the McCaslins whose saga Faulkner finds he is writing this time.

"Was" opens *Go Down, Moses* before Isaac's birth, and the title story, from which he is also absent, closes the saga. That tale concerns the execution of Tomey's Turl's great-grandson, Samuel Worsham Beauchamp. Butch Beauchamp had been a bad egg in Jefferson, a numbers runner, and finally a murderer in Chicago. The gist of the tale has to do with his grandmother Mollie Beauchamp's wish that he be brought home for his funeral and the designs by which the lawyer Gavin Stevens, a character newly introduced in this last story, arranges for the body's return. If "Was" gives a naïf view of antebellum life as carefree comedy, with an easy fraternal feeling between the McCaslin twins and their blacks, "Go Down, Moses" closes the parentheses around Isaac's life by showing a McCaslin Negro as an alienated criminal executed in a distant northern city. A vestige of the communal feeling of Southern life remains as Stevens inveigles the local editor and merchants on the square to join him

13. James Early, *The Making of Go Down, Moses* (Dallas, 1972), 16–19.

and the aged white lady whose grandfather had owned Mollie's parents in raising money to ship the body home, hiring a hearse, and providing flowers.

Like "Was," this tale is jarringly out of key with the story-chapters intervening between them, the first with its farcical comedy, the last with its bleak view of modern life. What such disjunction among its parts suggests is that *Go Down, Moses* is a chronicle, bearing a relation to the novel observant of the unities like that of Shakespeare's *Antony and Cleopatra* to *Hamlet* or *Lear.* We are shown the South into which Isaac McCaslin is born, the timeless wilderness and then the family history into which he is initiated, and the society that lives on after him. Each of Faulkner's novels differs in its form; each is an experiment, an enlargement of what the novel can do. Faulkner has never limited himself to following the dimensions, structure, or shape of what the novel *was,* for his interest in each book is to make the experience of fiction represent what the novel *is.* And while what *is* includes "grief or sorrow," it includes also the admixture of comic literary stereotypes with folklore, inverting its sources, analogues, and influences to produce a tale at once a comic masterpiece and a fitting prelude to the darker themes in *Go Down, Moses.*

SINS OF THE FATHERS

If *Go Down, Moses* is a novel, what is its structure? As a dynastic chronicle it ranges in time from 1851 ("Was") to 1940 ("Delta Autumn" and the title story), with many flashbacks among the intervening years. The reader's attention is shifted from character to character; Uncle Buck and Uncle Buddy, protagonists of the first tale, do not appear again until Part 4 of "The Bear." The time of the second tale, "The Fire and the Hearth," is contemporary, about 1940, and its chief character is Lucas Beauchamp, a black grandson of old Carothers McCaslin. "Pantaloon in Black," the third story, concerns a Negro lumber-mill worker named Rider; not related to the dynastic family, he is a Mc-

Caslin tenant who idealizes Lucas and Mollie Beauchamp's marriage. Many critics consider this tale an interpolation in *Go
Down, Moses;* I make a case below for its intrinsic place in the
structure of the novel.

The next three tales have as their central character Isaac
McCaslin. In "The Old People," he is a boy of ten to twelve, initiated into the ritual of the hunt by the part-Indian, part-Negro
guide Sam Fathers. "The Bear"(1883) takes place in Ike's six-
teenth year, and develops the strangely twinned themes of the
hunt for and eventual death of the great bear who is the spirit of
the wilderness, and Isaac's exploration of the plantation ledgers
kept by his father and uncle. In "Delta Autumn" Ike is eighty
years old, returning for a last hunt in the diminishing forest;
here he endures the realization that despite his own gestures of
renunciation and expiation, his family's original sins are being
reenacted unto the fifth generation. The final tale concerns the
execution of Lucas and Mollie's grandson.

Of the seven tales, five are short stories of 25 to 35 pages, but
two—"The Fire and the Hearth" and "The Bear"—are novellas
of, respectively, 102 and 144 pages. Although the theme of race
relations is inextricably woven into this saga of the fates of both
white and black descendants of Carothers McCaslin, the only
tales with black protagonists are "The Fire and the Hearth" and
"Pantaloon in Black." (The central character in "Go Down,
Moses" is not Butch Beauchamp—he is already dead—but
Gavin Stevens.)

Faulkner's way of giving his novel structure is to juxtapose its
parts and its characters to emphasize relationships between
them by repeated parallels and contrasts. For a start, we may
consider the two tales whose length sets them apart from the
rest. In "The Fire and the Hearth" we see the McCaslin inheritance as experienced by Lucas Beauchamp, the black grandson of
the original begettor, while "The Bear" explores the inheritance
of Carothers' white grandson, Ike. Because the two novellas are
so different in style and feeling most readers may not perceive
their parallels. Apart from one intense and nearly tragic episode,
Lucas' tale is told in the comic mode, carrying forward the folk-

lore themes and tone of the preceding story, "Was"; "The Bear," on the other hand, continues the ritual and epic style of the tale preceding it, "The Old People," and, as noted, develops the tragic theme of historical knowledge.

Contrasts can prove as significant as parallels. If we compare what we know of Lucas with what we know of Ike, we see how Faulkner has devised our comprehension of the multifold and complex fate of the McCaslins in these complementary life stories in both races, and how he has given *Go Down, Moses* a structural integrity to hold its constituent tales together in one network of interconnections.

Both Lucas and Isaac are most strongly moved by their sense of honor, a conviction each sees as inherited from Carothers McCaslin. For Lucas, honor demands that he dare confront his white cousin and landlord, Zack Edmonds (who is Carothers McCaslin's grandson too, by female descent), for after the death in childbirth of his wife Zack had preempted Lucas' wife Mollie as wet nurse for his newborn son and had kept her living in the big house for six months. After getting Mollie back, Lucas is still so enraged by Zack's insult to his honor that he tries to kill the white man, knowing that his own reward will be the lyncher's rope and the bonfire. Isaac, on the other hand, equally moved by *his* sense of honor, experiences its demands in a different sphere of action: he must take upon himself the burden of his family's guilt, distributing to his black cousins the bequests of one thousand dollars each left them by their grandfather; and, more than that, honor demands that he expiate the McCaslin sins by renouncing his own inheritance. To do so Isaac loses his own wife, for he values honor in this matter above his love for her or hers for him—human love, for Isaac, is subsumed, it seems, in the lusts of the body. Impervious to his wife's sexual temptations, Ike refuses the tainted inheritance he needs to support her and any children they might have had. Instead, "uncle to half a county and father to none," he takes the wilderness as his true bride, the wilderness into which he was initiated by Sam Fathers.

In contrast to Ike's asceticism, Lucas' attitude to married love is indicated by the symbolism of the title of his tale. Calling

Lucas' story "The Fire and the Hearth" signals the centrality to his life of the fire he had lit on his wedding night, "which was to burn on the hearth until neither he nor Mollie were left to feed it" (47). In his youth, confronting Zack, Lucas reveals the depth of his passion; in his age (during the rest of the novella he is sixty-seven), his mad infatuation with buried treasure tempts him to abandon Mollie but in the end love overcomes this aberration.

Lucas regards Ike's renunciation of his inheritance as a sign of weakness; he himself makes no such renunciation. When he turned twenty-one (in "The Bear"), he promptly presented himself to Ike, demanding his thousand dollars. In "The Fire and the Hearth," Lucas is not only farming his land but making money on the side with a moonshine still. While hiding the still in the woods he finds a gold coin in an old Indian mound, and the rest of the tale involves his search for the buried treasure of which he takes the one coin as proof.

The plot of each novella involves a hunt—more than one, in fact. Lucas hunts for buried treasure, Ike for the big bear Ben and for the significance of his family's ledgers. Although these hunts are parallels, the tone in which they are given makes for contrasts. Lucas' treasure hunt is the very stuff of comic fiction, preceded in the telling by another farcical episode involving moonshine stills and the bumbling efforts of young George Wilkins, suitor to Lucas and Mollie's daughter Nat, to win Lucas' consent to their marriage. In his treasure hunt Lucas is both the tricked and the trickster. He succumbs to the lure of a divining machine sold by a white travelling salesman; to purchase it, he steals one of Roth Edmonds' mules. This he must retrieve, and after further skulduggery Lucas salts a deserted orchard with his own fifty silver dollars, takes the salesman there to find a few coins, and so tricks him into renting for twenty-five dollars per night the finding machine the salesman should well know is worthless. The theme of buried Confederate treasure is a staple of Southern folk tradition, one that Faulkner had used before in *The Unvanquished* and *The Hamlet*; the salted mine is another familiar motif.[14] But where Flem Snopes had used this trick fraudulently to entice Ratliff and his friends to buy the Old Frenchman's Place and pitilessly had driven poor Henry Armstid mad, in "The Fire and the Hearth" when Lucas buries his own silver dollars in the orchard he is merely getting his own back in a sequence of comedic actions untinged by Flem's moral squalor.

The treasure hunt is followed by further comedy, Mollie's deciding to divorce Lucas because the gold he seeks is evil, forbidden by the Bible, and Roth Edmonds' taking the two to court, where the divorce proceeding is halted at the last gasp by Lucas' belated recognition that no buried treasure is worth the break-up of his forty-three-year marriage. In contrast to these shenanigans is the ritualistic and epic grandeur of Isaac's hunts in the wilderness and the *gravitas* of his search of the ledgers. In Ike's story, comedy preceded his birth, in "Was"; in the three tales in which he is protagonist he is fated to attain an ecstatic sense of union with the eternal forces of nature, and a knowledge of man's tragic fate. Comedy there is none.

When Lucas confronts Zack Edmonds to avenge the white man's taking Mollie, he acknowledges his own courage—like Zack's in facing him—as the result of his McCaslin blood, specifically his inheritance from Carothers. So when each grandson touches the bedrock of his being, Ike discovers in his McCaslin inheritance his burden, whereas Lucas finds in his not knowledge of sin but the source of his pride.

"The Fire and the Hearth" has affiliations with the preceding story, "Was," in the working out of this theme, as well as in the comic themes of treasure hunt and trickster. Lucas' confrontation of Zack, although an act of desperation for which he must

14. In the files of the Mississippi State Department of Archives and History, Jackson, this motif appears in items collected from Panola County by Merle N. McCurdy (Record Group 60, Box 121, No. 133) and from Granada County by Erle Johnson (No. 241-C). In the Mississippi WPA collection at the Library of Congress, A627, accession no. W918, collected by Mrs. P. C. Wilson, records a tale from a Choctaw informant about a ghost haunting the site of buried Confederate gold.

steel himself, is nonetheless conducted according to a code, the rules of the game as elaborate and as binding as those of the wagers and card games in "Was." Lucas waits for daylight before he enters Zack's bedroom because he declines to sneak up on an adversary in the dark. Once there, Lucas throws out the window the open razor in his hand, then dares Zack to draw his pistol, and lets him take the pistol out of the dresser, both knowing that Zack will not fire on Lucas unarmed. Instead Zack flings the pistol on the bed so both can have a chance to seize it. Earlier, Lucas had given Zack his chance to come get his infant son whom Mollie had brought to the cabin to nurse, but Zack, knowing Lucas would confront him, had not taken that gambit. Now the two kneel, "their hands gripped, [each] facing across the bed and the pistol the man whom he had known from infancy, with whom he had lived until they were both grown almost as brothers lived. They had fished and hunted together, they had learned to swim in the same water, they had eaten at the same table in the white boy's kitchen and in the cabin of the negro's mother; they had slept under the same blanket before a fire in the woods" (55).

Like Bayard and Ringo, like Henry Sutpen and Charles Bon, the black man and the white are in a symbiotic relationship, "almost as brothers." Where in *The Unvanquished* there is no conflict between them, and in *Absalom, Absalom!* the end is fratricide, here, when Lucas gains the pistol, fully intending to use two bullets, one on Zack, the other on himself, the gun misfires. Having shown Zack—and himself—that he had the guts to do the deed, Lucas does not try the gun again. His pride has been sufficiently assuaged, even though he knows that he cannot ever ask whether the white man has had his wife, and that if he were to ask, the white man would not answer. But no one has been killed, and life goes on.

Surrounding the intensity of these dozen pages, the comedy of trickery unfolds in the pursuit of buried treasure and, not so comically, in its corrosive effect upon love. Lucas saves himself at last by forswearing the divining machine. In this way he makes a renunciation after all that parallels and foreshadows

Ike's spurning of his tainted inheritance—with the significant difference that Lucas does so to preserve his marriage, not to abandon it.

EASY RIDER

Among the seven stories in *Go Down, Moses,* "Pantaloon in Black" is the seeming anomaly. None of its characters is a Mc-Caslin; what connects "Pantaloon" to the family chronicle appears tangential. Its central character, Rider, rents a cabin from Carothers McCaslin and emulates Lucas by lighting a fire on the hearth when he marries Mannie. But after only six months of marriage, Mannie dies; and the tale tells of Rider's grief, his despair, his attempts to lose himself in his work, in drink, and his inviting his own death by committing a murder. The last part of "Pantaloon" is spoken by a deputy sheriff to his wife; this white man can't understand "them damn niggers. . . . Because they aint human . . . when it comes to the normal human feelings and sentiments of human beings, they might just as well be a damn herd of wild buffaloes" (154).

Failure to find "Pantaloon in Black" an integral part of *Go Down, Moses* is only one of the problems this story has posed for some readers. Another is objections of varying sorts to the characterization of the black protagonist and the action. Walter Taylor finds the plot a Gothic cliché, recalling "Poe's familiar dictum that 'the death . . . of a beautiful woman is . . . the most poetical topic,' and should be told through her 'bereaved lover.'" Further, Faulkner's tale "can only disappoint" the reader who seeks "some genuine sampling of the sense of Negro life," for "Faulkner never truly gives shape to the deeper workings of Rider's mind," relying instead "on mere clichés" ("Rider carries a razor, drinks 'moon' whiskey," eats "greens, cornbread and buttermilk"). "The heart of the problem . . . is that convincing dialect . . . can be a means of avoiding deeper characterization."[15]

15. Walter Taylor, "Faulkner's Pantaloon: The Negro Anomaly at the Heart

Rider is indeed a bereaved lover, and it is on the quality of his love, rather than on his dialect or his diet, that our attention should be fixed. As depicted by Faulkner, Rider is remarkable for the intensity of his feelings. His name, and the title of his tale, bring into play some associations that seem germane to our understanding. Calling the story of a tremendously strong Negro lumberjack "Pantaloon in Black" is a typically Faulknerian oxymoron, since "Pantaloon" suggests the buffoon of pantomime, but the treatment of Rider is serious. Only the deputy sheriff finds the bereaved lover ridiculous, a point of view the tale itself presents as insensitive and uncomprehending.

We assume Rider to be the character's given name; family name he has none. It has been suggested that Faulkner derived this name from a widely known blues song, "Easy Rider," and its cognate blues, "I Know You Rider" or "Circle Round the Sun," with the repeated refrain, "I know you rider, gonna miss me when I'm gone." H. R. Stoneback proposes "that we consider this song as a kind of objective correlative for the prose-poem 'Pantaloon in Black,'" but goes on to term the function of the tale within the novel to be "essentially non-novelistic."[16] This last observation I think mistaken.

As I have suggested above, Rider's devotion to Mannie is consciously modelled upon what he perceives as Lucas' to Mollie. Like Rider, Lucas was twenty-four when he dared threaten a white man to regain his wife, whose love the fire on the hearth symbolizes. And Lucas is not the only other twenty-four-year-old husband in these stories. George Wilkins, too, is just that age, secretly married to Nat; but where George is so shiftless that after six months he has yet to mend his sagging porch and build a proper well, Rider, by contrast, "in just six months . . .

of *Go Down, Moses,*" *American Literature,* XIV (November, 1972), 438–40. This article is condensed in Taylor's book, *Faulkner's Search for a South* (Urbana, 1983), 139–40.

16. H. R. Stoneback, "Faulkner's Blues: 'Pantaloon in Black,'" *Modern Fiction Studies,* XXI (Summer, 1975), 241–45, *vide* 242.

had refloored the porch and rebuilt and roofed the kitchen, doing the work himself" (137).

When Mannie dies, Rider's first impulse after her funeral is to return to their cabin. One of his fellow workers tries to assuage his grief with an offer of "a jug in de bushes" and, when Rider persists, tries to restrain him: "You dont wants ter go back dar. She be wawkin yit." For "everybody knew" about "the dead who either will not or cannot quit the earth yet" (136).[17] It is strongly to be inferred that what keeps Mannie's spirit lingering by the smoldering hearth is that either Rider's love for her, or hers for him, or that of each for the other, is so lasting that she cannot help but stay by him. Then, as he attempts to reassure her— "Hit's awright. Ah aint afraid. . . . Wait. . . . Den lemme go wid you, honey"—she fades from his sight. "He could actually feel between them the insuperable barrier . . . of the blood and bones and flesh too strong, invincible for life" (140–41).

The rest of Rider's story tells how he tries to rejoin his dead wife's spirit. In his grief he rejects food, the comforting of family, and the consolation of religion. He tries to lose himself, first in work—single-handedly heaving a huge log onto the truck—and then in drink. He seeks out and joins the ring of black men being fleeced in their weekly dice game with Birdsong, the white night watchman. In what appears to be a gambling brawl but in fact is his willful committing of an act he knows will bring about his own death, Rider exposes Birdsong's cheating and, as the white man reaches for a pistol, he slashes Birdsong with his razor. Just as the rigged game repeats but despoils the motif of the gaming table in "Was," this confrontation repeats that between Lucas and Zack, the black man with razor, the white with gun; but this time the struggle is not between brothers in blood or in spirit, and there is no intercession of the rules of a code, no throwing aside the razor or evenhanded grappling for the pistol.

17. "The most common view . . . is that the spirit . . . stays around the house (or visiting loved places and friends) for three days after the . . . death and then stays around the grave for three days more" (Newbell Niles Puckett, *Folk Beliefs of the Southern Negro* [Chapel Hill, 1926], 86).

Rider kills Birdsong with a single swipe. The rest of his story, the death he sought and now awaits, is told in another voice, that of the incredulous deputy.

If, as I think, the main relevance of Rider's story to the rest of *Go Down, Moses* has to do with his all-but-superhuman devotion to Mannie, counterpointed as that is to the love of Lucas and Mollie which Rider idealizes, and the less satisfactory marriage of George Wilkins to Nat Beauchamp, then we may well compare Rider's passion that leads him beyond the grave to the behavior of another lover later in the book: Roth Edmonds, in "The Old People." Roth (Zack's son, the baby suckled by Mollie Beauchamp after his mother's death), now grown, is a member of a hunting party that includes old Ike McCaslin. This is long after the death of the bear, and the woods are shrunken. Another in the party makes broad hints about Roth's hunting a doe. At last Isaac comprehends when, the hunters having set off without the old man, a handsome young woman turns up in camp, carrying an infant swaddled in a blanket. Roth had left with Isaac an envelope in case he should receive a messenger, and the message to be given is "No." This is a woman with whom Roth had lived, and the child is his. When the woman lets slip that her mother had taken in washing, Ike is jolted by the awareness that she is "a nigger"; in fact she is the great-granddaughter of Tomey's Turl. Ike thus sees that Roth Edmonds has repeated Carothers McCaslin's original sin, the seduction of his Negro kinswoman; as the envelope contains money Roth would give her, he commits also Carothers' blood-payment for the sin of (in this case remote) incest. Should we remember, as Faulkner intends that we do, Rider's devotion so intense that he tried to follow his wife's ghost into the otherworld, then sought oblivion and finally a death in which to join her, we see that Faulkner implies here, as in the Dilsey section of *The Sound and the Fury*, that the blacks in Yoknapatawpha are capable of qualities of love unattained by the whites, despite, or perhaps because of, their lives of suffering, their lack of sophistication and worldly advantages.

THE LAST OF THE CHICKASAWS

"The Old People" introduces Isaac McCaslin and Sam Fathers in a scene that invokes the biblical language of the creation of the world: "At first there was nothing. There was the faint, cold, steady rain, the gray and constant light of the late November dawn." Into this void of space and light "with the voices of the hounds converging somewhere," Ike, with Sam at his shoulder, then sees that "the buck was there. He did not come into sight; he was just there, looking not like a ghost but as if all of light were condensed in him and he were the source of it" (163). This is the language of sacrament, of vision; although the buck is "not a ghost," that Ike sees him, kills him, and is initiated into brotherhood with both the slain buck and all the hunters—Sam's ancestors—who have gone before, vouchsafes to him a vision later in the tale. This is the sight of another buck, huge, also not a ghost but a real beast, yet one whom only the spiritual initiate is qualified to see.

The boy Ike is tutored in the ways of the woods and its creatures by the old master hunter Sam Fathers. Like every other significant character in the Yoknapatawpha saga, Sam has a genealogy; a condensed version is given in a discursus of several pages just after Ike has pulled the trigger on that first buck. Sam is the natural son of Ikkemotubbe, the Chickasaw chieftain, and a Negro slave descended from an African chief. Sam is now the last remaining member of the tribe; ostensibly the blacksmith on the McCaslin place, he did hardly any work, nor heeded the commands or desires of any of the whites. There had been another Indian, Jobaker, with whom Sam spoke the old tongue. When Jobaker died Sam told McCaslin Edmonds: "I want to go to the Big Bottom to live. . . . Let me go." His phrase echoes Ike's earlier imploring Cass to "Let him go," reflexive of the spiritual that gives the book its title. Cass had explained to Ike that Sam "was born in the cage . . . he knows nothing else"; betrayed by his mother's black blood, he was "himself his own battleground . . . the mausoleum of his own defeat" (173, 167–68). But Cass misreads Sam's character, for Sam never loses his dignity or his pride. As the last of the Chickasaws he gives Jobaker's body the traditional cremation, then returns to the hunting ground of his ancestors, living in the big woods in solitude until the arrival each November of Major de Spain and the hunting party.[18] The only other character with Indian blood is Boon Hogganbeck, a genial, loyal man with the mind of a child. Boon's grandmother was a Chickasaw (his grandfather's winning her hand is told in the story "A Courtship"). Although Boon is a white while Sam is considered a black man and lived among the Negroes when on the plantation, Boon defers to the son of Ikkemotubbe since his own Indian blood was not that of a chief.[19]

The poignance of Sam Fathers as the last of the Chickasaws invokes Cooper's Uncas a century earlier. Faulkner goes to some lengths, however, not to present the Chickasaws as Noble Savages. While treating their religious beliefs, as he understands and re-creates them, with great respect, Faulkner does not exempt his Indians from the taint of humanity, original sin. Just as the McCaslin history starts with the sins of Carothers, the Indian inheritance begins with those of Ikkemotubbe. He is the cousin of the reigning chief; after an absence of seven years during which he sowed wild oats in New Orleans among the French, he suddenly reappears and, as Thomas Sutpen will do a generation later, makes his bold bid for power. With the ruthless cunning of an emperor in *I, Claudius*, Ikkemotubbe arrives with a vial of poison powder and murders his way to the throne by killing the young son of his frightened cousin, who quickly abdicates in his

18. The Chickasaw practice, however, was not cremation but burial beneath the floor of the log house, "the family continuing to live there" (Frank G. Speck, "Notes on Chickasaw Ethnology and Folk-Lore," *Journal of American Folk-Lore*, XX [1907], 57–58).

19. Among Chickasaws, "Descent is counted in the female line" (*ibid.*, 52). But for Faulkner descent is always dominant in the male line. Lucas Beauchamp's thoughts of his ancestry center on his grandfather Carothers McCaslin; of his grandmother Eunice or his parents, Tomey's Turl and his wife, we hear nothing.

favor. Not for nothing does Ikkemotubbe call himself "Doom" (the English pronunciation of the alleged French translation of his name, "Du Homme").[20]

We should not assume that Ikkemotubbe adopted slavery from the whites, for the black slave upon whom he begets Sam is his own. In historical fact the Chickasaws, an "unconquerable" tribe of warriors, enslaved their captives from neighboring tribes and maimed their slaves' feet so that although they could work they could not flee. Black slaves arrived after 1720 bearing the goods of English traders from Charleston; some escaped harsh white masters and fled to the Indians; others were purchased by the Chickasaws.[21] After Sam's birth Ikkemotubbe marries the woman off to another Indian (hence Sam's name, Had-Two-Fathers), and sells mother and son to Carothers McCaslin. Doom had already sold the land to Carothers, in defiance of the Indian custom of communal proprietorship of land which no individual could possess.

So Ikkemotubbe commits the same sins as Carothers. He owns slaves, he has sexual relations with his slave woman, he disowns his half-black son, and he presumes to ownership of the land in violation of a sacred trust. If the Chickasaws ever were Noble Savages it was before history began. The wilderness itself is prelapsarian; human society, even that of the Indians, defiles it.

Ikkemotubbe's callousness in disowning and enslaving his own son makes Sam's lot parallel to that of Carothers' son, Tomey's Turl, while Sam's being made to endure the status of the unprivileged race in his mixed blood resembles the lot of

20. "I know it's *de l'homme* . . . it seemed righter to me that Ikke., knowing little of French or English either, should have an easy transition to the apt name he gave himself in English, than that the French should be consistent" (Faulkner to Malcolm Cowley, October 27, 1945, in Cowley, *The Faulkner-Cowley File: Letters and Memories, 1944–1962* [New York, 1966], 43). So the mistaken French is attributed to the Indian, not to the author.

21. Arrell M. Gibson, *The Chickasaws* (Norman, Okla., 1971), 40–42; Lewis M. Dabney, *The Indians of Yoknapatawpha: A Study in Literature and History* (Baton Rouge, 1974), 8–10.

Lucas Beauchamp too. Yet again, as the inheritor of such knowledge of his father, his situation resembles that of Ike in Part 4 of "The Bear," learning the truth of his grandfather's sins.

Sam Fathers' (and Boon Hogganbeck's) inheritance is more fully developed in the short stories grouped under the heading "The Wilderness" in *Collected Stories* (although there are some inconsistencies between them and *Go Down, Moses*). As Lewis Dabney has shown, some of the characteristics given in *Go Down, Moses* as Chickasaw in reality pertain to the Choctaws, the enemy tribe who lived to the South.[22] Indeed, in Faulkner's story "A Justice" the Indians were Choctaws, becoming Chickasaws in "Red Leaves," "A Courtship," and "Lo!" "The Indians actually were Chickasaws, or they may be so from now on," Faulkner explained to Malcolm Cowley; " 'Red Leaves' actually were Chickasaws. 'A Justice' could have been either, the reason for their being Chocktaws [*sic*] was the connection with New Orleans, which was more available to Chocktaws," and he sketched a map showing how the Tallahatchie River bisected the two tribes' domains.[23]

Sam Fathers manages to evade the doom of being Doom's son by becoming a priest of the wilderness. We know Sam is a priest because, when Ike has pulled the trigger and his first buck has fallen, Sam acts not as only a hunting instructor: "The boy . . . drew Sam Fathers' knife across the throat and Sam stooped and dipped his hands in the hot smoking blood and wiped them back and forth across the boy's face. . . . the first worthy blood which he had been found worthy to draw" (164–65). This is a *rite de passage*. In fact Ike has now passed two such rites: killing the buck—" 'Did he do all right, Sam?' his cousin McCaslin said. 'He done all right,' Sam said"—was a secular rite, marking his graduation from boyhood. But the anointing of the first-time hunter with the blood of his kill was a sacred tie, one that joined

22. *E.g.*, Faulkner drew on a description of "the Choctaw funeral, in which the body was placed on a platform, as is Sam Fathers" (Dabney, *The Indians of Yoknapatawpha*, 37).

23. Faulkner to Cowley, December 8, 1945, in *The Faulkner-Cowley File*, 66–67.

him and Sam Fathers "forever, so that the man would continue to live past the boy's seventy years and then eighty years, long after the man himself had entered the earth as chiefs and kings entered it" (165). Son of a chief, Sam exercises a spiritual power, and the power of its transference; but this power differs in kind from the raw domination and murderous manipulations of his father Ikkemotubbe.

At the end of "The Old People" the hunters break camp and are about to return to Jefferson, but Sam, becoming aware of an approaching buck, halts them. Boon, Walter Ewell, Sam, and Ike set out in its pursuit. Ewell is the most skillful hunter among the townsfolk, a technician of the secular. When, after long pursuit and Ike's halting in the woods where Sam tells him to stop, they hear the clap of Ewell's rifle and the blowing of his horn, Ike assumes that once again Ewell has bagged the game. But Sam motions him to be silent.

Then the boy saw the buck. It was coming down the ridge, as if it were walking out of the very sound of the horn which related its death. It was not running, it was walking, tremendous, unhurried. . . . Then it saw them. And still it did not begin to run . . . passing within twenty feet of them, its head high and the eye not proud and not haughty but just full and wild and unafraid, and Sam . . . his right arm raised at full length, palm-outward, speaking in that tongue which the boy had learned from listening to him and Joe Baker in the blacksmith shop. . . .

"Oleh, Chief," Sam said. "Grandfather." (184)

Walter Ewell, meanwhile, stands puzzled over the yearling one-point he had shot as it lies beside tracks too huge for it to have made. The huge buck is both a real beast and a totem, to be seen only by the spiritually worthy.

When Sam addresses the buck we know he is not merely a skilled hunter but one who is himself a shaman. Thus it is that Sam knows better than anyone where the game is, what the deer or bear will do, where they will go, for his spirit is kin to theirs. And so he knows, hearing Walter Ewell's rifle, that the great buck had not been hit and would in a moment appear before him.

Among the Chickasaws, a "common ceremony . . . is the transfer of the shamanistic practice from a shaman to an aspirant," the anthropologist Frank Speck observed in 1907. "The real shamanistic power, however, can be obtained only from a class of spirits called *l'yacanacá*, 'people of his clan,' meaning, in the broadest sense, his ancestors, who are known to dwell as spirits abroad in the woods. They are invisible to all but those having a shaman's power."[24] That Ike is able to see the buck whom Sam addresses as "Chief. Grandfather," attests to his having passed the first stage of the initiation for which Sam has trained him, and which Sam had marked by streaking his face with the blood of his first kill. His elder cousin Cass had come this far before him; this far but no further. Cass is a good man, he empathizes with the cyclical processes of the natural world (as he tries to explain them to Isaac at the end of "The Old People"), and when Ike insists that he saw the buck, Cass tells him that he too had seen the buck—it must have been sixteen years before, since he is that much older than Ike—when Sam brought him into the woods after his first kill.

But Sam chooses Ike, not Cass, for the further stages of initiation into his shamanistic knowledge and power. This must be because Sam has an intuitive sense of Cass's spiritual limitations, made explicit when he objects to Ike's staying in the woods after Sam's death, and General Compson admonishes him: "You've got one foot straddled into a farm and the other foot straddled into a bank; you aint even got a good hand-hold where this boy was already an old man long before you damned Sartorises and Edmondses invented farms and banks to keep yourselves from having to find out what this boy was born knowing and fearing too maybe but without being afraid" (25). Ike's worthiness as Sam's acolyte had been intimated by his response to the wilderness, "profound, sentient, gigantic and brooding," where until he had taken part in its process of death renewing life, he had felt "dwarfed" and "alien" (176). He feels instinctively his kinship with the wilderness spirit, not a transcendental and passive spectatorship of its power and majesty but an active partici-

24. Speck, "Notes on Chickasaw Ethnology and Folk-Lore," 56.

pation in its cycles of life and death while deeply acknowledging its majesty and power.

In his reading of Faulkner under the spell of deconstructive critical theory, John T. Matthews maintains that

The time of the "old people" and the space of the wilderness' communal ownership are created in the novel only under the auspices of Sam Fathers' fictions, and not through any wilderness mystery cult. . . . Isaac's career in the forest also teaches him . . . that the practice of these rites by civilized men is a kind of speech or writing; they are art rather than magic, substitution rather than repossession, translation rather than annulment. In this second respect, Isaac is initiated by Sam Fathers into a society of authors, whose words create a past that never was, whose articulations are the nearest approach to original plenitude, and whose language is dedicated to the rites of mourning.[25]

Such may be the effect of "The Old People" or the whole of *Go Down, Moses* when read by a French philosopher, but how adequate a description of the reader's actual felt experience of the characters' experience is such a translation of fiction into a wordplay divorcing described action, because described, from any cultural or historical context? It is as though Faulkner wrote in a sealed room without reference either to the burdens of history—the very theme of his work—or to his own experiences as a member of the annual hunting parties that camped in General Stone's deep woods. Fiction reduced to abstract wordplay from which the historical imagination is exiled can have no greater moral depth than do fantasy tales or science fictions whose connections to actual life are at best tangential. To make Sam Fathers the president of a wilderness chapter of P.E.N., to deny that the rites he practices, the folkways he imparts to Ike, the history of his people that Ike absorbs and feels himself continuing, possess either mystery or any connection to a society, is deeply to mistrust the authorial power of fiction and to misread this book. It is unmistakable that the society of the Chickasaws is here re-

25. John T. Matthews, *The Play of Faulkner's Language* (Ithaca, 1982), 216, 244.

duced to a population of one, Sam, who by initiating Ike into its mysteries doubles its membership. But it *is* a cult, the practice of which is necessarily conducted by speech if not by writing, as truly for primitive as for civilized man, for how else is culture maintained and passed on?

Matthews' statement, however, that this language "is dedicated to the rites of mourning," a point he makes about the language of all of the stories in *Go Down, Moses,* is on the mark. He responds eloquently to the elegiac quality of the entire book, with its repeated efforts to arrest time, to keep alive by the acts of remembering and writing the immitigably transient, trying to halt the disappearance of the past by resurrecting its memory. If we accept the present as embodied in the action of this tale, we see the process in operation as Ike tries to halt the transitoriness of living by the intensity of his remembering. As the wagon jolts through the woods after the breakup of the camp, "the wilderness watched them pass . . . never to be inimical again since the buck still and forever leaped, the shaking gunbarrels coming constantly and forever steady at last, crashing, and still out of his instant of immortality the buck sprang, forever immortal" (178).

This passage anticipates Cass's invocation, in "The Bear," of Keats's "Ode on a Grecian Urn" to explain to Ike the meaning of his experience. There it serves as trope for the whole tale, indeed for the novel, as we shall see. Suffice it here to say that the arresting of time in the words of a fiction makes possible our repossession of the past; but to maintain, as Matthews does, that "words create a past that never was" is to detach memory from reality. That the reality is imagined does not deny its function, its actuality, in our suspension of disbelief; the imagined past is the creation of the author, but to the character to whose imagination it is attributed it is reality itself. To think otherwise is to strip from literature its power to move us. For if the past of "The Old People" and the rest of the Yoknapatawpha saga "never was," how can we read it with such fascination, or regard Faulkner's interpretation of the past as an imagined version of what Henry James called "the complex fate" of being an American?

As Sam Fathers tells the lore of his tribe to Ike, Faulkner writes:

as he talked about those old times and those dead and vanished men of another race . . . gradually to the boy those times would cease to be old times and would become a part of the boy's present . . . as if they were still happening. . . . And more: as if some of them had not happened yet but would occur tomorrow, until at last it would seem to the boy that he had not come into existence yet, that none of his race nor the other subject race which his people had brought with them into the land had come here yet . . . and that it was he, the boy, who was the guest here and Sam Fathers' voice the mouthpiece of the host.   (171)

In passing on his heritage to the boy, Sam initiates Ike McCaslin into his tribe as a shaman in his turn. After Sam's death, Ike will indeed be the last of the Chickasaws.

DISPOSSESSED OF EDEN: "THE BEAR"

No matter that it began as yet another tale about Quentin, or that the famous colloquy in which the boy hunter hears "Ode on a Grecian Urn" was originally between Quentin and Mr. Compson. No matter, either, that the hunting story was at first a tale about the love of a man for his dog—Boon Hogganbeck and Lion.[26] From these early versions, published in magazines, it is evident that Faulkner had within him for years the germ of his greatest novella, and that its themes haunted him, as did those of his other tales and novels, until, after several tellings, at last he got it right. The final telling of the tale is thick with implication, reverberant with meanings that extend backwards and forwards throughout *Go Down, Moses.* Many readers have found these meanings problematical, contradictory, unresolvable; others have resolved them, but in ways with which not everyone can agree. I shall advert to some of these interpretations, but

26. Early, *The Making of Go Down, Moses,* 31–32. "Lion" and the first version of "The Bear" are reprinted in *Uncollected Stories of William Faulkner,* 184–200, 281–95.

first I wish to summarize the tale, give it context, explore its derivations, and reflect upon its significance.

At the time when Faulkner was writing "The Bear" he was reading *Moby-Dick* aloud to his daughter Jill.[27] Not surprisingly, there are resemblances between the greatest hunting tales of the American nineteenth century and of the twentieth—resemblances, and significant differences as well. In each there is the hunt, by a variegated crew, of a totem beast, a creature larger than life, one that represents the very essence of nature. In both works the actual hunters of this beast are members of primitive races (Queequeg, Daggoo, Tashtego; Sam Fathers, Boon Hogganbeck) seeming to hunt at the behest of their masters, who can be seen (in *Moby-Dick*) to represent capitalism, or (in "The Bear") the society of status, property, power.

In *Moby-Dick* it is still possible for Melville to imagine Nature as overpowering man; the whale, though hunted, is not slain—indeed he exacts revenge upon Ahab and his crew, of whom Ishmael alone survives to tell the tale. In "The Bear," although the wilderness into which Ike McCaslin is initiated is magisterial and the big bear Old Ben awe-inspiring in his strength and wiliness and courage, the wilderness nonetheless proves frangible. Already there is a logging train that chugs through the forest, and on Ben's death, Major de Spain sells his tract to the lumber company, and the exploitation and destruction of a wild domain as old as time is swiftly accomplished.

Further, there is a fundamental difference between the Pequod's hunt of the great white whale and "the yearly pageant-rite of the bear's furious immortality" (194). The polyglot international crew headed by American mates serving New England investors pursues the whale from the profit motive, for which Ahab, in his wounded rage and pride, substitutes his own agenda of private vengeance upon the malignity of the universe that has maimed him. Thus in both its economic origin and its development as a rebellion against the gods, the hunting of Moby-Dick is clearly different from the pursuit of Old Ben.

27. Blotner, *Faulkner: A Biography*, II, 1054.

Faulkner's hunters enact a white men's sporting ritual that adapts to the ends of leisure-class recreation what for the Indians had been a necessity and a mystical experience. We must bear in mind that in "The Bear" the hunters are of two groups; on the one hand there are the aristocrats who when in town embody the power structure of their society—General Compson, Major de Spain, McCaslin Edmonds, Walter Ewell—and their black servants, the cook Uncle Ash and Tennie Beauchamp, who tends their horses. On the other hand there is Sam Fathers, whom they regard as their half-Indian, half-black guide, but who, as we know from "The Old People," and from his having often seen Old Ben but never having shot him, is in fact a shaman reenacting each November a sacred rite on his ancestral hunting ground. Although the boy Ike is heir to a plantation, he treads the woods with the watchful reverence that Sam has instilled in him. Then there is Boon Hogganbeck, the quarter-Chickasaw white man, big, brave, loyal, dim-witted. He does the bidding of others, runs errands for the Major, can't even shoot a squirrel, but it is he who actually kills Old Ben.

Two years after the death of the bear Ike McCaslin returns to the hunting ground. Everything is changed now, for civilization—the railroad, the loggers, the exploitative destruction of the wilderness—already encroaches upon the virgin land. It is evident that Old Ben was far more than merely a beast to be hunted; he was somehow the embodiment of the spirit of the wilderness.[28] With the bear's death, the wilderness itself is doomed. This is prefigured in the passing of Sam Fathers; at the moment Old Ben is slain, Sam falls to the ground in a seizure from which he does not recover. Ike and Boon stay behind to care for Sam when the rest of the party returns to town, and at his death they inter him as he had desired, in the fashion of his Indian ancestors.

In the fifth section of the tale Ike is aware, on his return, that the locomotive is now the dominant image of energy and motion in the woods. Why does Ike return? He comes back to make

28. Bear is one of the animal deities or totems among the Chickasaws reported in Speck, "Notes on Chickasaw Ethnology and Folk-Lore," 55.

a pilgrimage to the hallowed places where the wilderness spirit
has enfolded him, where Lion is buried, where Sam Fathers lies.
At the graveside of the tutelary Master of his boyhood, Ike has
an epiphany of the immortality of all life. The tokens he had left
on Sam's grave—the twist of tobacco, the bandanna, the pepper-
mint candies—these things, Ike knows, are gone,

> not vanished but merely translated into the myriad life which printed
> the dark mold of these secret and sunless places with delicate fairy
> tracks, which, breathing and biding and immobile, watched him from
> beyond every twig and leaf until he moved, moving again, walking on
> . . . quitting the knoll which was no abode of the dead because there
> was no death, not Lion and not Sam: not held fast in earth but free in
> earth and not in earth but of earth, myriad yet undifferentiated of every
> myriad part, leaf, twig, and particle.   (328)

This vision of Ike's makes him aware of the eternity of the
processes of nature, the energy of life encompassing death and
translating it, restoring the vigor of their spirit to all perished
things. Such a consolatory view of Nature as the mother of life is
more like the animism of Indian belief than the Christian concept of immortality. Although Ike is the truest Christian in
Faulkner's tale (as we see in Part 4), he is at the same time the
one true follower of Sam Fathers the Chickasaw shaman. In the
midst of this reverie on the immortality of all that is mortal, Ike
is awakened by an intuitive fear: at his feet a rattlesnake slithers
across the forest floor, pausing to raise its head by his knee. Con-
fronted by this serpent, "the old one, the ancient and accursed
about the earth, fatal and solitary . . . evocative of all knowledge
and an old weariness and of pariah-hood and of death," Ike, without premeditation, raises one hand, as Sam had done when the
boy had shot his first buck, and, "speaking the old tongue which
Sam had spoken that day without premeditation either: 'Chief,'
he said, 'Grandfather'" (329–30).

This I find one of the most touching, the most nearly unbear-
able moments in American fiction, so beautifully has Faulkner
embodied the elegiac celebration of the vanishing wilderness, as
well as the mystical realization of Nature that runs through our

literature from Thoreau to Robert Frost and beyond. The serpent is only residually the Christian emblem of man's temptation and Fall. This snake appears to Ike primarily as it would have to Sam, "who had been his spirit's father if any had, whom he had revered and harkened to and loved and lost and grieved" (326); indeed the snake comes to him as the temporary vessel embodying the spirit of Sam Fathers, his ancestor and his immortality. In both the mythology of the American Indian and the folklore of the Negro, the snake is a figure of deific stature and mysterious supernatural power.[29] Faulkner is being profoundly true to mingled strains in Sam Fathers' blood in giving his spirit this mortal form.

There is only another page or two to the story. Ike pushes further into the woods until he comes upon Boon, frantically hammering his gun barrel with one of its dismembered parts. Boon is screaming; "Get out of here! Dont touch them! Dont touch a one of them! They're mine!" (331) as a maelstrom of squirrels leaps from branch to branch in the tree above him. The mighty bear slayer is reduced to this hysterical claimant of ownership over squirrels. When Ike had asked Major de Spain's permission to revisit the hunting camp, the Major having reserved from his sale to the lumber company a small plot including the campsite, de Spain had wished him luck and said, "If you have it, you might bring me a young squirrel" (317). Major de Spain has repeated Ikkemotubbe's original sin of selling the land, and in the camp where Ben was hunted there's no longer even luck enough to bag a squirrel. On this note of moral diminution and pathos ends the greatest American hunting tale of the twentieth century.

29. Speck (*op. cit.*) reports Snake as another Chickasaw animal totem or deity. The snake that survives repeated sheddings of its skin is a symbol of immortality. Puckett wrote that the python deity was worshipped in the Ewe territory in Africa, "and this vodu cult, with its adoration of the snake god was carried to Hayti. . . . Thousands of Negroes from these serpent-worshipping tribes were . . . carried across the Atlantic. . . . At the same period, Ewe-speaking slaves were taken to Louisiana" (*op. cit.,* 177–78). Planters fleeing with their slaves to Cuba during the Haitian revolt against France were again displaced by the French-Spanish war in 1809, bringing their slaves, "faithful adorers of the serpent," to New Orleans (181).

"The Bear" is at once so simple and so complex that it surrenders its meaning to the conscious mind only after repeated readings and much brooding. Yet it communicates its significance instantaneously, although we may not at once be able to restate that meaning. As Eliot has said of poetry, it can be appreciated before it is consciously understood. One reason why this is true of "The Bear" is that the events of the plot correspond to several of those patterns of behavior which are intrinsic to our cultural experience, indeed may be a part of the biological inheritance of man. The Hunt in this tale is at once a Pursuit and a Quest. The Hunt of the Sacred Beast, a divine totem, is perhaps the most ancient in the repertoire of human stories. In whatever form, whether in an epic poem like *Gilgamesh*, an allegory like the hunting of the unicorn, a saint's legend like that of St. George and the dragon, a novel like *Moby-Dick*, or a tall tale like Thomas Bangs Thorpe's "The Big Bear of Arkansas," the pursuit of the supernatural beast defines the world of Nature and of man. The huntsman who succeeds in this pursuit is marked for life and immortality as a culture hero, a deliverer of his people. Faulkner's "The Bear" conforms to this general and universal pattern, but only up to a point. The differences as well as the affinities of Isaac McCaslin with the kind of hero we expect from such preternatural hunting tales signify our comprehension of his role and of Faulkner's achievement.

The Hunt, however, is only one of the archetypal patterns in the tale. This hunt is also a Quest, for a more spiritual way of life than the common lot of our ordinary days. Isaac is the designated hero of this quest, seeking, in the first three parts of the tale, to discover the ultimate truths according to the guidance of Sam Fathers, in an unmediated relationship with Old Ben, the spirit of the wilderness. In Part 4 he must seek his truth in the world of men, coming into knowledge of his familial inheritance of guilt.

Considering together the themes of Hunt and Quest we find that they include still another fundamental human pattern: that of Initiation. In a very primitive sense this story is a Coming of Age ceremony for Ike McCaslin. The Hunt is the first stage of his Initiation; his realization that the Hunt is in fact a Quest is what we may call the second stage. The third stage is played out in Part 4, where he is initiated into knowledge of evil. The final stage is his attempted expiation of the sins of his fathers.

These patterns of Hunt, Quest, and Initiation give "The Bear" much of its intuitive power. Whether such patterns are, as Carl Jung maintains, inherent archetypes of the human psyche, or whether they are the structures of myth to which our culture gives a reflexive response, they operate upon the reader to make the actions of the tale seem larger than the events and lives in which they take place. Further, these basic patterns are fused with other conflicts and tensions characteristic of American life. Indeed, the mythic and ritualistic actions are deeply imbedded in conflicts that define the great crises of American history—the tensions between wilderness and civilization, between the Red Man's ethic and the White Man's exploitative way of life; the conflict between freedom and slavery; and between instinctual, pagan values and Christian obligations, between unfallen freedom and knowledge of sin.

The slaying of Old Ben is conventionally interpreted as the self-destroying fulfillment of Major de Spain's hunting party. But in fact Ben is not killed by any of the hunters from town, despite their years of trying. Sam Fathers knows that "Somebody is going to, some day," kill the bear, and Ike agrees "That's why it must be one of us," the initiates, "So it wont be until the last day. When even he dont want it to last longer" (212). Sam knows that it will take a dog larger, braver, more savage than the hunting hounds Old Ben has been raking at will, and it is Sam himself who discovers the fated beast, Lion, in the woods, and trains him—he can't be tamed—so that he can be made to hunt with the men. Lion is as wild a beast as Ben himself, and the only human beings he permits near him are Sam and Boon. In fact Lion prefers Boon, whose nature is more nearly savage like his own, and sleeps on Boon's pallet. In the end, when Lion attacks Ben and the bear encloses him in a loverlike embrace, crushing the guts and the life out of him, their struggle is not so much a hunt as a part of the endless killing and being killed of nature itself, the eternal symbiosis of the slayer and the slain. While the two wild creatures are locked in fatal struggle, Boon, distraught at the damage done to Lion, leaps upon the bear and with his pocket-knife bores into the creature's body, severing the life in him. This attack by Boon replicates that in *Moby-Dick* by Ahab, who, like an "Arkansas duellist," had tried to slay the whale with a bowie knife. Where Ahab failed, however, Boon succeeds in killing the beast that represents the spirit of Nature.

Boon does the bidding of his civilized betters, does it mindlessly, enacting with his giant's strength and childlike devotion to Lion, his soul mate, the ritual slaying that Sam Fathers had foreseen and foretold. How had Sam known when Ben must die? How but that as a shaman his wisdom included foreknowledge of the coming destruction of the wilderness; for now that he, Sam, the last living Chickasaw, is old and childless, his days and the days of his people and of the wilderness they reverenced are coming to an end. So Sam knows that Old Ben soon must die in heroic struggle with a fellow beast, cannot be driven to an ignominious death by the sportsmen from town and the squatters and railwaymen who cluster to the camp to see the final hunt. Like the critter in Thorpe's "The Big Bear of Arkansas" a century before, Ben was "an unhuntable bear."[30] His carcass was found to contain fifty-eight bullets that had failed to bring him down, even as Moby-Dick had trailed the lines of futile old harpoons. Like Thorpe's Big Bear, Old Ben "died when his time come."

In Part 4 of the tale, we move from the Red Man–White Man world of the hunting party into the tangled self-examination of the White Man–Black Man world, the plantation. But the plantation was founded in the wilderness, originally the home of the

30. Thomas Bangs Thorpe's "The Big Bear of Arkansas" was first published in *Spirit of the Times* in 1841 and was widely reprinted then and since, *e.g.*, in Walter Blair, *Native American Humor* (New York, 1937), 337–48, and in Kenneth S. Lynn (ed.), *The Comic Tradition in America* (Garden City, 1958), 127–37. Comic yarns about bear hunts were a staple of the popular antebellum magazine *Spirit of the Times*; several are reprinted in Arthur Palmer Hudson (ed.), *Humor of the Old Deep South* (New York, 1936), 109–19; these are broadly comic, but none approaches the exuberance and grandeur of Thorpe's "The Big Bear of Arkansas."

Red Man, and, as we have seen, the aboriginal Red Man Ikke-motubbe had already practiced slavery and miscegenation, and sold his birthright, the land, to the original White Man, Caroth-ers McCaslin. Ike's contemplation of the old plantation ledgers, illiterately kept by Uncle Buck and Uncle Buddy in cryptic lines he must decode, reveals the continuation of these original sins by Carothers, who inherits the Indian's sins, as it were, as cod-icils to his property deed.[31] Grandfather Carothers bought more slaves and, in the most culpable denial of another person's lib-erty, seduced his Negro servant Eunice. This sin he compounded twenty years later by seducing the daughter Eunice had borne him. With such guilt Carothers McCaslin, the recusant Scots-Presbyterian, could live, but the double shame of her own seduc-tion by her master and his incest with their daughter was too terrible for Eunice to bear. On Christmas Day, 1832, she com-mitted suicide by drowning herself in the river.

Similar, if lesser, sins of greed and lust are evidenced on the

31. The McCaslin brothers' ledger seems fanciful indeed, but in fact keeping such a journal was customary. In *DeBow's Review* (New Orleans) for June, 1851, under the heading "Management of Negroes Upon Southern Estates/Rules and Regulations for the Government of a Southern Plantation,/by 'A Mississippi Planter,'" among other regulations appeared the following:

> The overseer shall keep a plantation book, in which he shall register the birth and name of each negro that is born; the name of each negro that died, and specify the disease that killed him. He shall also keep in it the weights of the daily picking of each hand; the mark, number and weight of each bale of cotton, and the time of sending the same to market; and all other occur-rences, relating to the crop, the weather, and all other matters pertaining to the plantation that he may deem advisable.

(Reprinted in Bruce Jackson [ed.], *The Negro and His Folklore in Nineteenth-Century Periodicals* [Austin, 1967], 348). Such a plantation book, kept by Dr. Martin W. Philips of Magnolia and Oxford, was published as "Diary of a Missis-sippi Planter, January 1840 to April 1863" in *Publications of the Mississippi His-torical Society* (1909), where Faulkner may have read it. Joseph Broguner, who proposes this possibility, mentions its "focus upon the personal lives of the slaves" and "traces of the 'serviceable syntax' of the McCaslins' ledgers and of similar cryptic entries" ("A Source for the Commissary Entries in *Go Down, Moses*," *Texas Studies in Literature and Language*, XIV [1972], 545–54; quota-tions from 546–47).

distaff side of Ike's family too. His uncle Hubert Beauchamp is discovered to have had sexual relations with a freed Negro girl on his place, and his greed is revealed when Isaac, aged twenty-one, opens the burlap bag in which Hubert had sealed a silver cup filled with gold pieces as a bequest at Isaac's birth. The generous uncle had borrowed back his own bequest to cover losses at poker, and had substituted for it a tin coffee pot filled with copper pennies and—now that he is dead—unredeemable IOUs.

But if the McCaslin sins prove graver than those of Hubert, there are in the family—in the blood, Faulkner would say—attempts to make expiation. Old Carothers would not admit, lacked the moral courage to acknowledge, his offenses to those he had wronged, yet he made a partial, posthumous gesture of responsibility, as Ike discovers, decoding Uncle Buddy's painful scrawl: his will left a thousand dollars to each of his Negro grandchildren, to be given on their coming of age. "*So I reckon that was cheaper than saying My son to a nigger,*" Ike thought. "*Even if My son wasn't but just two words. But there must have been love . . . Some sort of love. Even what he would have called love: not just an afternoon's or a night's spittoon*" (169–70). Ike, in his innocence, cannot but with difficulty conceive of a nature as lustful and callous as that of his grandfather. Ike is dismayed by Carothers' brutal indifference, and tries to imagine the circumstances of his seduction of Tomasina, his own daugher by Eunice: "perhaps he had sent for her at first out of loneliness." But nothing can assuage the horror—"*His own daughter His own daughter. No No Not even him*" (270). After such knowledge, what forgiveness?

In the second generation of McCaslins, as we have seen in "Was," the expiatory gesture was much more a personal acknowledgment of responsibility than was Carothers' posthumous money deed. Uncles Buck and Buddy, before Buck's marriage, had, on Carothers' death, offered freedom to their slaves, moved into a log cabin they had built themselves, and turned the great house over to the blacks as a dormitory. The brothers recorded the evidence of their father's debauchery, apparently not fully comprehending it themselves although their manumission of the slaves suggests they knew of it. But it is left to Isaac fully to understand the familial guilt and most fully to try to expiate it.

Ike's renunciations differ more in degree than in kind from the expiatory gestures of his father and uncle. We may observe, too, that gestures of selflessness and generosity, though none is sufficient to atone for the sins of history, are a part of the ethical code of the very class responsible for history's burdens: the Southern aristocracy, as Faulkner presents it. We see a lesser instance of this spirit of *noblesse oblige* in Major de Spain's invitation to the squatters, who have shot his game and trespassed and farmed on his property, to take part in the hunt and share in the spoils. We see it again in McCaslin Edmonds' assumption of the debt to Isaac of the birthright cup of gold coins Isaac's uncle Hubert had bequeathed and then denied him. This spirit of *noblesse* appears in the cameraderie of the hunting camp, where the strict hierarchy of classes in town is suspended for the fortnight in the woods. There General Compson and Major de Spain acknowledge that the pride of Uncle Ash, the old black cook, requires that he, too, be permitted to hunt with the white men after Ike, a mere boy, had killed a buck. It is evident in their dealings with all their kith, kin, and servants, whether white, black, Indian, or mixed in blood, that these men, in Faulkner's view, are like the Knights of the Round Table in their unfailing courtesy. The hunting party with its male cameraderie and earned distinction is associated in their mind with their service in the Confederate Army, another Quest, another romantic lost cause.

Such generosity of spirit is found among the leaders and is the reason they are respected by the plebeian members of their society. If, in Faulkner's work, a man who has assumed the moral prerogatives of leadership proves not to possess the requisite largeness of spirit, he has betrayed a sacred trust. It is such a betrayal that makes fitting the death of Thomas Sutpen in *Absalom, Absalom!* at the hands of Wash Jones, the poor white whose daughter Sutpen had seduced in hopes of begetting a male heir and had abandoned when the baby was born a girl. In "The Bear" there are no such ignoble leaders. But none of the aristocrats makes such renunciatory and expiatory gestures as does Ike. If they are the princes of this world, their generosity flawed by their unacknowledged implication in our common fallen state, Isaac McCaslin is clearly the nearest among them to a higher principality.

This story of "the heart's driving complexity" takes its place in the tradition of, and in part derives from, another tale of a Southern boy's discipleship to a black man and initiation into the irremediable evils of the white man's world. Huck Finn is apprentice to Jim as sorcerer; for it is Jim who had knowledge of the supernatural, is adept at divination, knows the charms and spells, and is in touch with the majesty of nature.[32] In *The Adventures of Huckleberry Finn*, Huck and Jim, too, are "dispossessed of Eden," their Eden being the natural world on Jackson's Island, and as they drift down the river of history on their raft, at every landfall Huck learns lesson after lesson of the depravity of "the damned human race." The evil of slavery is a given in this book: Jim has already suffered forced separation from his wife and children and runs away to escape being sold downriver himself; but in the novel the only further evidences of oppression Jim suffers are thoughtless pranks at the hands of Huck (on the raft) and Tom (on the Phelps plantation), and the condescension of the Duke and Dauphin. In the corruption, the evils—Pap's brutality, the vindictiveness and cowardice of the lynch mob, the greed and venality of the Duke and Dauphin, the horror of the Grangerford-Shepherdson feud—all of the victims are as white as the perpetrators. Mark Twain attacks not slavery alone but human nature itself; yet his despair is everywhere leavened by irony, by a comic imagination almost wholly absent from "The Bear." Further, while Huck actually participates in or is present as witness to the experiences of man's wickedness, Ike must re-create his heritage by imagining what his grandfather had actually done. The consequences of those deeds comprise the present life of the McCaslin plantation and, by extension, of

32. I have examined this in detail in "Black Magic—and White—in *Huckleberry Finn*," Chapter 15 of *Form and Fable in American Fiction*.

the South; the introspective complexity of narration—the disruptions and evasions of sequential time, the oneiric quality of the prose in the fourth part—"creates the real by dreaming how it will eventually be remembered."[33]

In recent years "The Bear" has been reinterpreted by critics who bring to literary analysis the methods, predilections, and assumptions of other disciplines. The deconstruction of literary texts, applying to literature abstract principles derived from linguistics, has deprivileged the texts so analyzed in much the same way that the reliance on linguistic methodology nearly a century ago subordinated literary values to searches for ur-versions. Other current vogues include reader-response criticism, in which the text is created not by its author but by its reader; Marxist and other varieties of criticism applying economic determinism to the production of literary works; and, in the wake of the civil rights movement, criticism of literature, particularly the writings of a Southerner like Faulkner, with a sense that its chief value will be determined by its treatment of racial themes.

It will be inferred that these recent approaches are determinedly secular. For instance, John T. Matthews, in his deconstructive study *The Play of Faulkner's Language*, observes, *inter alia*: "Sam seeks to initiate Ike into the special tongue of those who have discovered how to read and write the wilderness, a tongue indecipherable to others, such as Walter Ewell, who could 'swear there was another buck here that I never even saw. . . .' The early portions of 'The Bear' present Isaac's discovery that the hunt is an aesthetic imitation of death and loss rather than a mythic celebration of their transcendence."[34] If one denies vision and reduces transcendent experience to mere authorship the story is indeed demystified, except that other mysteries arise—such as why Walter Ewell couldn't see the Great Buck. If the bear hunt is for the character experiencing it (rather than the reader reading about it) only "an aesthetic imitation of death and

33. R. W. B. Lewis, *The Picaresque Saint* (Philadelphia, 1959), 204.
34. Matthews, *The Play of Faulkner's Language*, 252.

loss," there is of course no way that the reader, too, can find it "a mythic celebration of their transcendence." But consider the contrary case: if, as I have maintained, to Ike the hunt is indeed a participation in a ritual sanctified by generations of Sam Fathers' forebears, then the spiritual refreshment that flows from the hunt's taking of life is inevitable, not only for him but also for us who vicariously participate in his experience. It is possible that the inability to believe in such experience follows from readers and critics never having known anything like the wilderness in which Faulkner places Ike at the moments before and during its vanishing.

Economic determinism leads interpretation away from the text, from the emotional logic of what the text actually says, in other ways. A recent anthology of critical discussions of Faulkner, Richard Brodhead's *Faulkner: New Perspectives* (1983), widely used as a textbook, includes, as its essay on the present work, Susan Willis' "Aesthetics of the Rural Slum: Contradictions and Dependency in 'The Bear.'" This is an able presentation of the conflicts in the tale, but it does reflect its own dependency upon "dependency theory," an interpretation that presents "the underdevelopment of the Third World as a direct result of contact with capitalism" and "defines the historical contradictions of domination in terms which can then be related to the form and language of the literary text." Willis convincingly argues "the spatial juxtaposition of two wholly distinct worlds: the wilderness and the commissary," and the opposition in the tale between the narrative modes of myth and of document; but only to an economic historian does it follow that "The truth of the text's two worlds is a dialectic between unequal modes of production." Further, she confuses Faulkner's invocation of the wilderness with "the wilderness community," as though the hunting party were the repository of the same values as those revered by the aboriginal Chickasaws; thus she can say, offering as proof Ike and Boon's trip to Memphis to buy whiskey for Major de Spain, "The recognition of a direct link between the wilderness and the centers of commerce explodes once again the myth of nature and its illusory isolation," as though the transcendent values Sam and Ike associate with Old Ben and the wilderness express economic dependency upon Memphis. She concludes that "Myth in Faulkner is a direct expression of dependency."[35]

It would be hard to make a case for dependency as the cause of myth in such works as *A Fable, Light in August, The Unvanquished,* and *The Hamlet,* where the tension between "wilderness and the centers of commerce" is nonexistent. In "The Bear" Willis restricts "myth" to the wilderness passages, evidently exempting from consideration as myth Ike's imitation of Christ (examined in Chapter I) and his entire participation in the Quest as an Initiation. "Myth" seems to signify, for Willis, only the hunting of the bear, not its effect upon the chief participant in the action; only the wilderness venue, not the participation in that setting of the white boy who has become the inheritor of the shaman's visionary knowledge. Nevertheless Willis, whose reading of other aspects of the tale is astute, concludes that "The Faulknerian world is not an organic unity, but a tormented disunity," though one need not agree with the rest of her sentence—"inscribed within the oppression of dependency."[36]

Economists of necessity must face unresolved tensions, and so are more tolerant of them than are literary critics whose rage for order impels them to try to wrestle disparities into some kind of unity. Such critics are sorely tempted to bring within the iron bonds of a single explanation the turmoil and conflicts in a work that may have been intended by its unresolvability to represent the complexity of our experience. Eric Sundquist's passionately argued *Faulkner: The House Divided* "defines aspects of Faulkner's novels on racial conflict" and maintains that "the three great novels"—*Light in August, Absalom, Absalom!* and *Go Down, Moses*—derive from Faulkner's "discovery of a theme emblematic of the combined passion, fear, and promise of racial conflict—the problem of miscegenation." Sundquist's readings of the first two novels are convincing; in *Go Down, Moses,* he

35. Susan Willis, "Aesthetics of the Rural Slum: Contradictions and Dependency in 'The Bear,'" in Richard J. Brodhead (ed.), *Faulkner: New Perspectives* (Englewood Cliffs, N.J., 1983), 174–75, 138, 184.

36. *Ibid.,* 174.

maintains that "the conjunction of incest and miscegenation . . .
is once more revealed . . . as the heart of the South's long, continuing catastrophe." But what has this theme to do with the
wilderness? "[T]he stories drive toward, and fall away from, the
revelation of grief in the act of incest and miscegenation that co-
incides with the sacrificial death of the totem animal. Those
two acts have a relationship charged with paradoxical significance." In *Go Down, Moses,* then, the themes of "the tragedy of
race," "the Calvinist rhetoric of damnation," and "the violence
of racial hatred" associated with "the terror of incest" are intrin-
sically connected "to a third American theme, the sacrifice of
the totem animal. That conjunction . . . depends . . . on the continued insistence of commentators both more or less 'racist' in
their points of view that the Negro is a 'beast' psychologically,
emotionally, socially, or in every conceivable way."[37] On the
grounds that Faulkner's work emerges from and reflects a background of racial antagonism in popular culture, Sundquist offers
as proof his analysis of a once-popular novel, *The Sins of the Fathers* (1912), by Thomas Dixon, author also of *The Klansman.*

Thus Sundquist arrives at the metaphoric interchangeability
in *Go Down, Moses* of shooting a buck or a bear in the woods
and seducing a slave on the plantation. The Negro is subliminally regarded as a beast, a King Kong to be hunted by proxy
when pursuing deer or bear; miscegenation is popularly assumed
to be the result of Negro men attacking white women, not of
white men violating black women. If Sundquist's argument that
miscegenation and hunting are equivalent images is true, it
must be so throughout the South and throughout Faulkner's
work. In *Go Down, Moses* hunting is also presented in the
comic mode; for Sundquist "the transition between comedy and
tragedy holds [the stories] in suspended antagonism . . . often defined by varying perspectives taken toward questions of sexual
power or legitimacy."[38] So then, we infer, Sophonsiba's being

37. Eric Sundquist, *Faulkner: The House Divided* (Baltimore, 1983), ix, 131,
137, 139.
38. *Ibid.,* 133.

presented by Hubert (in "Was") as "a Buck-hunter" would make Buck McCaslin represent the feared Negro, although she desires him; the actual fox Buck and Buddy pursue should also be, metaphorically, a Negro. Elsewhere in Faulkner, say in the early story "The Liar," Ek's being pursued by his father as though he were a bear (so that he can be forced to wear shoes now that he has turned twenty-one) signifies that Ek really represents a Negro; the hunt, then, is an image of miscegenation, although there are no black characters in the tale.

Sundquist's insistence on this presumed significance ignores the actuality of hunting, for its own sake, as a common American folkway. Incontestably, when Joe Christmas, a putative black who has slashed his white lover's throat, is pursued, we have the hunting of a Negro regarded as a beast. But it cannot be said of Old Ben that he is a beast regarded as a Negro, although Sundquist holds that "Both the hunt and the hysteria of racial fear displace the lust and violence of the subject onto the subject of sacrifice."[39] This point might be valid had Ben been killed by the white hunters who futilely pursued him for so many years; but, as I have suggested, the bear's death struggle with Lion and Boon comes, so to speak, as the fulfillment of Sam Fathers' shamanistic prophecy and represents the inexorable turning of the wheel of history—the supercession of the wilderness by the commercial exploitation of the land, the displacement of the Red Man's reverence by the White Man's greed.

Sundquist, although one of his avowed purposes (in which on the whole he succeeds) is to situate Faulkner's great works in their historical context, pursues a psychological rather than a cultural explanation of the hunting chapters. "The explicit sexual overtones of Ike's hunting of both deer and bear support . . . analogy" to Caddy Compson's virginity having to be destroyed to have existed at all in Quentin's mind, "just as the blood consecration, which links Ike to animal mother and surrogate father alike, represents in its own way the paradoxical violence in which the act of love may be expressed." I find that *just as* a false

39. *Ibid.*, 143.

binder; it falls apart on inspection; the animal blood connects Ike not to a mother but to the spirit of the buck, a male animal, that he slew, and to the spirits of his predecessor hunters, the Chickasaw men from Sam Fathers on back through the generations of time. For Sundquist, however, "There is, moreover, no other way to account for Ike's assertion that there must have been 'some sort of love' between Carothers McCaslin and the daughter whose child he fathers than to see it as desperately attached to the ritual of the hunt; that love, particularly that love, must for Ike have been destroyed in order to have existed at all."[40] Nowhere in the text can one find any such indication of a "desperate" attachment in Ike's mind of his grandfather's incest and his own shooting a deer or witnessing the death of the bear. Nor is there warrant for connecting the bear hunt to "some sort of love" that Ike, in his innocence, assumes Carothers must have felt for Tomasina—what we know of Carothers suggests little of such delicacy of feeling. That the violence of miscegenated incest and of the hunt are "desperately attached" is the fiction not of Faulkner but of the critic who wishes to bring into a single pattern the elements of a great work of literature he cannot otherwise unify.

On the final page of "Delta Autumn" Faulkner does make explicit the meshing of these metaphors, but their *enjambement* cannot signify the quarry's representing the bestial Negro in the South's phantasmagoric fear of miscegenation, as Sundquist proposes; for here the hunted creature is an image not of aggression but of victimization. On the way to the camp one of the hunters, Legate, has taunted Roth Edmonds for having hunted a two-legged doe the previous year; at the story's end Roth makes a kill that Legate describes as "Just a deer, Uncle Ike. . . . Nothing extra" (364–65). But Ike knows his kinsman has violated the code of virtue by abandoning the woman he had lived with and disowning their son, so he knows that Roth has killed a doe, violating the code of the wilderness and of the hunt. Sundquist's study is a valuable guide to *Light in August* and *Absalom, Absalom!*

40. *Ibid.,* 141.

but in discussing *Go Down, Moses* his forced argument contradicts the evidence of the text.

I do not maintain that *Go Down, Moses* is an unmediated replication of the chaos and emotional torment it explores. There is a way to receive the text as not disunified, while admitting its inexorably divided themes. I would propose that, to encompass the greater unity of the book within which its conflicts appear unresolved, we follow further the Quest and Initiation of Isaac McCaslin. The wilderness episodes are indeed juxtaposed to those in the commissary, the hunt *vs.* the ledgers, the timelessness of the eternal returns *vs.* the inexorable sequentiality of history. The main chance here is not to insist on equating the spilling of blood in the hunt with sexual violation and mixing of races but rather to examine what Isaac McCaslin learns from, and does, in both of the worlds of his experience.

As I have suggested, what Ike learns from his shaman is to seek purity by divesting himself in the wilderness of the appurtenances of human civilization, so that, by shedding his watch, his compass, his gun, he may be worthy to see the Great Bear and prove that his soul has shed its complicity in human guilt. I cannot sufficiently emphasize that for Ike, as for Sam, the purpose of the hunt is not to slay, but to *see* Old Ben: vision is the end, and the end is visionary. It is with this spiritual preparation that Ike reads the plantation ledgers; by renunciations he may achieve purity of spirit.

In his long discussion with his cousin Cass, who urges him not to renounce the proprietorship of the McCaslin plantation that history has made inevitable, Ike says that "Sam Fathers set me free" (300). What this means is that Sam had freed himself from his own corrupt inheritance by becoming a celibate priest whose bride was the wilderness; and when Ike, in his turn, must face the consequences, the burdens, of his own inheritance, it is Sam's path he follows in renunciation, poverty, and celibacy, having as little as he can manage to do with the tainted inheritance of his family and his fellow-men. In his search for spiritual purity, he could find, in the culture of the white South, no model as compelling as that of his Chickasaw preceptor. As for Sam, so for Ike "the woods would be his mistress and his wife" (326). Ike is the Grail Knight in Faulkner's Southern Quest. He had passed all of Sam Fathers' tests to become a witness of Truth from the Other World. But the truth Sam Fathers could bring him to was that of a world that was passing; after the death of the bear and Sam and the wilderness itself, Ike must bring his gifts to his own inheritance, his own world. He is not only a shaman, he is a Christian with full knowledge of original sin—and a Calvinist conscience.

"Let me go," Sam had asked when Jobaker died, leaving the McCaslin plantation for the deep woods. "Let him go," Ike had insisted to Cass. The lives of everyone, black and white and Indian, are animated by their efforts to achieve and enjoy freedom. Of this the title of the work should remind us. Many readers are misled by Mollie Beauchamp's application of the words of the old spiritual in the concluding story; "Done sold my Benjamin. . . . Sold him in Egypt" (380), she mourns, accusing Roth Edmonds of—what? The exile of her grandson, his criminal record, his execution? Accusing the white McCaslin of causing the sins and the sufferings of a black McCaslin. But the spiritual, though not explicitly mentioned or quoted earlier in the text, sends reverberant meanings throughout the tale:

> When Israel was in Egypt's land,
> Let my people go. . . .

In *Go Down, Moses*, Faulkner includes all the McCaslins, whites as well as blacks—indeed, whites more so than blacks—as comprising "Israel . . . my people"; "Egypt's land" is the South, the land of slavery, in which the oppressors are as oppressed as their slaves. Everyone in "The Bear" seeks freedom, but only Sam Fathers succeeds in finding it, if indeed even he does so. It is this theme, the search for freedom, the attempt to throw off the shackles of bondage, that in the end brings together the wilderness theme and the revelations of the ledgers in the commissary, and unites Ike as the last shaman of the Chickasaws with his role in *imitatio Christi*.

The stream of consciousness that characterizes Part 4 flows back and forth between Ike's efforts "to explain to the head of my family something which I have got to do, which I dont quite understand myself" (228), his reading and decoding the ledger entries, his reconstruction of the history of the South, his justifying his own renunciations, his search for his black cousin Fonsiba. With McCaslin, Ike explains his repudiations by interpreting Divine Providence. God, the Arbiter, sent the white men to the New World to start over, free of "that old world's corrupt and worthless twilight. He didnt condone" Carothers' sins, for because of them we have been "Dispossessed of Eden. . . . He ordered it and watched it"; He chose to supplant the Chickasaws with "another blood," and "He had foreseen the descendants Grandfather would have" (258–59). Isaac sees himself, then, as the instrument of Divine Will. When McCaslin, who interprets differently what the Book says, asks how we can know the truth, Ike replies, "The heart already knows . . . there is only one truth and it covers all things that touch the heart" (260).

The ledgers reveal that on Carothers' death Buck and Buddy tried to give their slaves freedom. "*Roskus . . . Freed 27 June 1837. Dont want to leave,*" nor did Fibby, Roskus' wife. Their son Thucydus, "*born Callina 1779. Rufused 10acre peace fathers Will 28 Jun 1837 Refused Cash offer $200 dolars from A. @ T. McCaslin 28 Jun 1837 Wants to stay and work it out* (266); in 1841 he accepts the "$200 dolars" and sets up as blacksmith. He had married Eunice, the woman Carothers seduced. The ledgers do not observe the freeing of the remaining slaves by the Emancipation Proclamation since this was not done by the McCaslins. But now that they are legally free, are they free in fact? Like the seekers of Jordan in *The Unvanquished*, "those upon whom freedom and equality had been dumped overnight . . . misused it . . . as human beings always misuse freedom" (293). Fonsiba's chosen fate represents the cruel irony of such "freedom"; she has married a Northern freedman and gone off to live on his 40 acres in Arkansas, though he knows nothing of farming. When Ike tracks her down to deliver her $1,000 bequest

he finds them starving, the man unable to stretch his government check to last the month. When Ike asks Fonsiba, who
stares at him without recognition, if she is all right, she replies,
"I'm free."

Isaac tries to tell her feckless husband, "This whole land, the
whole South, is cursed," and the best the whites can do is "maybe
just endure and outlast it until the curse is lifted. Then your
peoples' turn will come because we have forfeited ours. But not
now. Not yet" (278). There's no persuading this Northerner, his
head filled with liberal cant about "a new era . . . dedicated to
freedom, liberty, equality for all . . . this country will be the new
Canaan" (279), while he awaits the fruits of Canaan on his un-
tilled land.

Thinking of his remaining black cousin, Ike recalls that Lucas
had been named Lucius but changed his name (just as Faulkner
himself inserted the *u* in his surname) to create his own identity,
for "even he was repudiating and at least hoping to escape . . .
old Carothers' doomed and fatal blood which in the male derivation seemed to destroy all it touched" (293). Ike is convinced,
has convinced himself, that the blacks "will outlast us . . . will
endure. They are better than we are," for "their vices are vices
aped from white men or that white men and bondage have taught
them" (294), while their virtues—"Endurance . . . and pity and
tolerance and forbearance and fidelity and love of children"
(295)—are their own. Cass resists Ike's sentimental ennoble-
ment of the oppressed, but Ike insists that the black race had virtue "already from the old free fathers a longer time free than us
because we never have been free" (295)—and Ike's reverie floats
back seven years to an earlier colloquy with McCaslin, after Sam
had told Cass how he had rescued his fyce from Old Ben. Now
the themes of wilderness freedom and civilized enslavement are
braided together in Ike's remembrance of

an old bear fierce and ruthless not just to stay alive but ruthless and
proud enough of liberty and freedom . . . to put it in jeopardy in order to
savor it . . . an old man, son of a Negro slave and an Indian king, inheritor on the one hand of a people who had learned . . . pride through the
endurance to survive the suffering, and on the other side, the chronicle

of a people even longer in the land than the first, yet who now existed there only in the solitary brotherhood of an old and childless Negro's alien blood and the wild and invincible spirit of an old bear; a boy who wished to learn humility and pride . . . an old bear and a little mongrel dog showed him that, by possessing one thing other, he would possess them both; and a little dog, nameless and mongrel and many-fathered.

(295–96)

"*'And you didn't shoot,' McCaslin said.*" Ike was so close to the bear he could see "*a big wood tick just inside his off hind leg*" (296). This is the moment of epiphany, the boy without his gun between the paws of the totem divinity. And, as response, as interpretation, his cousin Cass, who has been like a father to Ike, takes a book down from the shelf and reads aloud "Ode on a Grecian Urn": "*She cannot fade though thou hast not thy bliss . . . Forever wilt thou love, and she be fair.*" Ike says the poet is talking about a girl; McCaslin replies: "*He had to talk about something. . . . He was talking about truth. Truth is one. It doesn't change. It covers all things which touch the heart— honor and pride and pity and justice and courage and love*" (297). Here Cass echoes what Ike himself had said about the heart's truth of the Bible, the Book that ordained their dispossession from Eden and his own appointment as the one to renounce the curse upon the South, the "doomed and fatal blood." So Cass, who had read the Book differently from Ike then, now offers the same proof of the heart's truth to validate Ike's transcendent experience.

But even this exposure to the heart's truth leaves unresolved the tensions it appears to have given resolution. Is it all explained "*in a book about a young man and a girl he would never need to grieve over because he could never approach any nearer and would never have to get any further away*"? The solace McCaslin has offered through Keats's poem is that memory, crafted into a work of art, can suspend the inexorable processes, the unassuaged desires, the uncompleted sufferings of life itself. The intensity of the remembered moment arrests time, as time had stopped when the boy Ike remembered seeing the Great Buck, or as now, when he relives the visionary moment in the presence of Old Ben, who can "never approach any nearer and would never have to get any further away" (297). The Grecian urn is by synecdoche an image of the entire ode, and for Faulkner an image not only of the bear, but also of "The Bear"—indeed, of *Go Down, Moses* in its entirety. For it is only in the mind's reconstruction of act, in the imagination of memory, that experience can be known, or the fated and irrevocable movement of history be transcended in the telling. In this is the triumph of permanence over flux, of art over life, of the timeless over time, of myth over history. Here, in the last of his great novels, Faulkner has reached back to the aesthetic of his apprentice years, so ill expressed in his feeble and fumbling verses: the Symbolist aesthetic, with its conviction of the sacredness of the poem, is invoked when the hallowed text, Keats's ode, speaks the heart's truth, Faulkner's story tells us, as that truth is spoken in His Word. By extension the book in which this sacred text is a central image also embodies "what the heart holds to": "*Courage and honor and pride, and pity and love of justice and of liberty*" (297).

Although almost all of Sam's tutelage passed on his Chickasaw sacred knowledge, Faulkner, in the passage recalling Ike's moment in the presence of the bear, emphasizes Sam's Negro blood and associates him with the blacks who inherited from Africa their knowledge of a freedom exempt from the corruptions of white civilization. Sam's blood is mixed, mongrel—as is that of the fyce, like him "mongrel and many-fathered." Lion, too, was a mongrel. Mixed blood, mingled races, thus appear as inherent goods, as the blood of the man and the creatures that frame Ike's transcendence in the wilderness frieze that represents his knowledge of freedom.

Recognizing his own divinely appointed role, Ike consciously imitates Jesus, "because if the Nazarene had found carpentering good for the life and ends He had assumed and elected to serve, it would be allright too for Isaac McCaslin" (309). Yet the evil, the inheritance, that Ike would repudiate is intractable. He knows that "the act of escaping (and maybe this was the reality and truth of his need to escape) was heresy: so that even in escaping he was taking with him more of that evil and unregenerate old man" Carothers (294), whose "doomed and fatal blood . . . seemed to destroy all it touched." When Ike marries the daughter of his house-building partner, she demands that he claim his inheritance and beget children. This he adamantly refuses to do. He will neither own the tainted land nor sire children to whom the sins and lusts of the fathers can be passed on. And so he lives, wifeless though unwidowered, childless, into the time when half the county calls him Uncle Ike.

The last of the Isaac stories, "Delta Autumn," shows that Ike's imitation of Christ is incomplete. His renunciations purify his own life but have no effect on anyone else's. Ike does not, after all, become the culture hero, the role that had seemed destined for one who passed the wilderness tests and was found worthy to approach the divine totem. Ike proves to be instead the failed culture hero, Percival, not Launcelot; the one who seemed chosen to redeem his country but fails to do so because of a human failing, a lack, ultimately, of compassion.

When Roth's abandoned mistress turns up in the hunting camp, Ike, now an old man, gives her the envelope of money Roth had left with him and the message, "No." This woman is so light skinned that Ike is filled with dismay and revulsion to realize, "You're a nigger." Roth had begotten a child upon the granddaughter of Tennie's Jim, the vanished brother of Fonsiba and Lucas Beauchamp. How shall Ike respond to this recrudescence in his family of Carothers' original sin—the miscegenation, the disowning of the child, the guilt money? In a voice that he "neither intended nor could stop"—an instinctual response—Ike tells her, "Go back North. Marry: a man in your own race. That's the only salvation for you—for a while yet, maybe a long while yet. We will have to wait. Marry a black man" (363). And as a last expiatory though futile gesture, he gives her, for the baby boy, the hunting horn left him by General Compson, a gift neither mother nor son will comprehend although to Ike it is a last tangible connection to his experience in the wilderness, his transcendence, his freedom: "This land . . . where cotton is planted and grows man-tall in the very cracks of the sidewalk, and usury and mortgage and bankruptcy and measureless wealth,

Chinese and African and Aryan and Jew, all breed and spawn together until no man has time to say which one is which nor cares. . . . No wonder the ruined woods I used to know dont cry for retribution! he thought: The people who have destroyed it will accomplish its revenge" (364). So he balefully muses, shivering in the cold rain after the woman leaves. Of all the facets of Carothers' sin it must be the miscegenation that most horrifies Ike, who here has a prevision of a whole land populated by mongrel peoples, white blood mixed with African and Chinese, Christian intermingled with Jew; and this mongrelization of America, of the South, will accomplish the retribution of the vanished wilderness.

Although Ike knew his spiritual guide Sam to be of mongrel blood, knew his fyce was a mongrel, Lion a mongrel, he cannot accept the mingling of his white McCaslin blood with Negro blood or, by extension, any such racial mixing. In part this is because miscegenation was Carothers' original sin and Ike cannot imagine repeating the mingling without repeating the sin. After all, in the South, with intermarriage a social anathema, the only way the races could be mixed would be by seduction and bastardy. Ike had told Fonsiba's husband the black people's turn will come "because we have forfeited ours. But not now. Not yet." And he tells Jim Beauchamp's granddaughter she cannot hope to marry a white man like Roth "maybe [for] a long while yet. We will have to wait." The convulsive overturning of laws and mores, of private attitudes and social organization, is deferred to a millennium, as far ahead as the Eden we are dispossessed from lies behind us. For the present, we must wait. Only in imagination, in a work of art like the Grecian urn, or in the remembrance of a time-stopped, eternal moment of transcendence, can Ike escape from the history in which he is doomed to live. He cannot know that the blacks whom he praises for their "endurance" will, in only a quarter century, cease to endure, will rise up in a nationwide movement that changes the laws and the mores of the country. For now, in 1940, Ike cannot by himself lift the curse on the South, cannot free himself of that curse, cannot imagine that it will soon be lifted. Not even his numinous experience in the deep woods saves him. Then, as Cass had said, he had known the heart's truth of "*Courage and honor and pride, and pity and love of justice and of liberty,*" the manly imperatives of the wilderness ethic. This ethic prepares him to commune with the sacred spirit of Nature, to grieve for the violated land, to mourn his people's enslavement to their own history, but it does not help him lift the curse.

"*Pity and love of justice and of liberty*" is not the same as love. And love cannot wait for the millennium. "Old man, have you lived so long and forgotten so much that you dont remember anything you ever knew or felt or even heard about love?" (363) Roth's abandoned lover reproves him. That wilderness ethic does not contain, along with its other virtues, *caritas*, as defined and required by Christianity. Sam Fathers' example led Ike to renounce rather than affirm his human ties in the pursuit of the transcendent—the wisdom of the ancient life of Nature—but this is not sufficient for expiating and forgiving the sins of life among men and women. Thus it is that Isaac McCaslin's imitation of Christ is incomplete.

Ike's predicament is Faulkner's own: while seeking freedom and redemption from his inheritance of the South, he is trapped in time. Writing the tales in *Go Down, Moses* between 1935 and 1942, the South Faulkner knew was still in the Great Depression, roads unpaved, farms tilled by mule-drawn plows, blacks and whites living in the poverty we today must study the photographs of Dorothea Lange and Walker Evans to imagine, the attitudes of these impoverished folk to their lot and to one another recorded in the still-unpublished files of the Federal Writers Project. Little hope, then and there, of the amelioration of their lot, or of the peaceful mingling of their genes. Intermarriage was unthinkable, an offense against custom and against law. Faulkner, no more than his fictional hero, could foresee the vast changes World War II and the consequent shifting of the black population northward would bring to the whole nation. Some critics have faulted Faulkner for not having foreseen the civil rights movement; by his townsfolk, however, during his lifetime he was much abused as a "nigger lover." As his Nobel acceptance speech makes clear, he deeply believed in human dignity; in his public statements as well as in his fiction he made plain that he included blacks among those dignified by their human- ity. His views on the race question, however old-fashioned the changes of the past half century have made them now appear, outraged many of his neighbors and alienated members of his own family. As a white Southerner, as a man of deep Christian faith, Faulkner felt that the guilt his region had to bear is the maltreatment during slavery and since of his black neighbors and kinsmen. His novels embody the anguish of his conscience, the complexity of the problem, and are at once unremitting in their honesty and triumphant in their literary fulfillment.

After *Go Down, Moses,* Faulkner continued his exploration of these problems, but with a considerable lessening of intensity. Each of his remaining books is a sort of sequel to one or more of the earlier ones. *The Town* and *The Mansion* round out the Snopes trilogy, but as suggested earlier, *The Town* is more a novel of manners than, as was *The Hamlet,* a powerful fable of archetypal actions and characters steeped in folklore. Ratliff, for one, dwindles into a busybody in the sequels. When he goes with Stevens to New York City and purchases a necktie from a Rus- sian émigrée, we feel that he, and we, have come too far from the travelling peddler who was the moral conscience in *The Hamlet.* There are occasional folktale subplots, as in the opening chapter of *The Town* (how Tom Tom and Turl, the two black firemen, turned the tables on Flem's scheme to blame them for his steal- ing the town's brass fittings), but these are only incidents along the way.

Intruder in the Dust (1948) and *A Fable* (1954) may be taken as sequels to *Go Down, Moses.* As I indicated earlier, in *A Fable* Faulkner contrives a literal allegory for the imitation of the life of Jesus, a theme more successfully because inferentially pre- sented in *Go Down, Moses.* In *Intruder in the Dust* Faulkner makes Lucas Beauchamp the central figure in a plot like that of a detective story: accused of murdering a white man, Lucas is in danger of being lynched by the victim's family. The lawyer Gavin

Stevens garrulously moralizes while an intricate plot unfolds. Compared to *Go Down, Moses*, the mingling of comic and tragic modes is disarticulated.

Requiem for a Nun (1951) resurrects Temple Drake from *Sanctuary* and, as her servant, Nancy Mannigoe from the short story "That Evening Sun" (both 1931), in a book whose nonce form consists of a three-act drama interspersed with narrative chapters providing history and background. The writing is talky and lacking in dramatic action, the development of theme allegorical. The sequel lacks the savage force of *Sanctuary*.

Faulkner's last book, *The Reivers* (1962), again reaches back to *Go Down, Moses* for the character Boon Hogganbeck, and to *Sanctuary* and *The Mansion* for the brothel keeper Miss Reba; the tale resembles also the interpolated fable in *A Fable* since *The Reivers* is a long farandole about a stolen racehorse. This is an amusing tale, told in a leisurely, relaxed fashion. It resembles *The Unvanquished* and *Go Down, Moses* in being the chronicle of a boy's initiation into life, but lacks the intensity of the earlier novels.

In these late works Faulkner is revisiting Yoknapatawpha County. That territory he had already deeply explored and thoroughly surveyed; there are few discoveries left to be made. The novels after 1942 are not built on the great structures of archetypal fables, nor do they deal so convincingly with the cultural inheritance of the South; neither do they draw upon the comic realism of folk tradition. When Faulkner's tales approach contemporary time the writing becomes noticeably shaky. Even in "Delta Autumn," Ike's preachments about how Americans will do in the coming war are shrill and jingoistic. The involvement of Eula's daughter Linda (in *The Mansion*) in the Spanish Civil War seems quite gratuitous and only detracts from the center of interest. Whenever Faulkner tried to cram contemporary news into his Yoknapatawpha saga, the headlines lack credibility. In the Compson genealogy, written for inclusion in *The Portable Faulkner* (1946), it verges on the unbelievable that Caddy Compson would have become the mistress of a Nazi general during the war. Faulkner's great subject was the past, the most powerful mode of his imagination, memory. His works have greatest power when he imagines the past as fable, when he brings before us lives whose acts and thoughts vivify the myths and folktales that deeply embody the inheritance of our culture.

INDEX